Praise for *Becoming Rooted*

"In a world sick with domination, striving, and consumption, Randy Woodley's *Becoming Rooted* offers a strong dose of very good medicine. Woodley speaks from his own big heart and his own profound story. He also gifts readers with wisdom from Indigenous peoples around the world to offer our divided and disconnected generation a way back to harmony. This is a must-read for everyone who longs for peace."

—Lisa Sharon Harper, president and founder of Freedom Road and author of *The Very Good Gospel* and *Fortune*

"I am grateful this book is in the world. As we hope to enter intentionally into a healing relationship with the Earth, Woodley's stories and reminders can inspire us to get there."

—Kaitlin Curtice, author of *Native: Identity, Belonging, and Rediscovering God*

"*Becoming Rooted* draws you deeper into relationship with the land where you live. Few of us live in the place we were born, but these reflections take you past that disconnection and help you notice the world around you in new ways."

—Patty Krawec, Anishnaabe author and co-host of the Medicine for the Resistance podcast

"Randy Woodley invites readers into the ancient and practical wisdom that has sustained the community of creation for generations. It is oriented toward deeply forming us into Indigenous ways of being, doing, interacting, and relating to one another and the Earth. The stories and examples provided are inspiring and compelling, drawing us out of the Western mechanistic logics that lead to ecological devastation and possible extinction and into Indigenous-oriented worldviews grounded in harmony and balance with all creation. In view of our current crisis, everyone should read this book individually and in a circle with others."

—Drew G. I. Hart, assistant professor of theology at Messiah University and author of *Who Will Be a Witness? Igniting Activism for God's Justice, Love, and Deliverance*

"*Becoming Rooted* offers us a precious way back into the land: a way into restoration and reciprocity, a way into healing ourselves and the land, a way of belonging again, a way of finding out who we are. Randy Woodley takes us by the hand and walks with us for the first one hundred days. We begin to think and feel differently, our senses gain new direction, and we start to gain roots. The law of the land becomes our most fundamental law, and we move as the land moves. After reading this book, we know enough to keep on the journey, to pay attention, to look and listen for the signs. Unless we become rooted, there is no future even for our next three generations. I am so grateful for this book and for the life and work of Randy Woodley."

—Cláudio Carvalhaes, associate professor of worship, Union Theological Seminary

"Randy Woodley reminds us that we all have an understanding of what it means to be indigenous to a spiritual place. Through slowly unfolding layers of meaning, he shows us where we may discover that place for ourselves."

—Steven Charleston, elder of the Choctaw Nation of Oklahoma, retired Episcopal bishop of Alaska, and author of *Ladder to the Light*

"During this season of complete disruption in our world, nothing seems more sacred and more helpful than a book drawing us to the land—the land God created and called good. Words, models, products, theologies, and practices can seem empty when surrounded by hostility and pain. We need a book that guides us to be better Earth dwellers, that apprentices us in the values God wrote into creation. *Becoming Rooted* is that book."

—MaryKate Morse, spiritual director, seminary professor, and author of *Lifelong Leadership* and other books

BECOMING ROOTED

BECOMING
ROOTED

ONE HUNDRED DAYS OF RECONNECTING
WITH SACRED EARTH

RANDY WOODLEY

BROADLEAF BOOKS
MINNEAPOLIS

BECOMING ROOTED
One Hundred Days of Reconnecting with Sacred Earth

Cover design and illustrations: James Kegley

Print ISBN: 978-1-5064-7117-4
eBook ISBN: 978-1-5064-7118-1

CONTENTS

INTRODUCTION

An Open Invitation

We must all get together as a race and render our contribution
to mankind.

—Redbird Smith, Keetoowah Cherokee, 1918

What does it mean to be rooted in the land? How are we shaped by
being from somewhere, some place, some land in particular? How
do we become rooted?

Indigenous people are those who originate naturally from a certain land, who have dwelled there for a long period of time. To be
Indigenous is to be rooted: to be part of a community or ethnic
group with historic continuity. Indigenous people understand how
to live with the land.

We are all indigenous to some place. We are all from somewhere. I repeat: we are all indigenous, from somewhere. Allow that
phrase to sink deep into your being. Now begin to open yourself
up to the reality embedded deep within your own DNA, your very
own identity. Each human being is a finely crafted amalgamation
of various ethnicities, each originating from a particular place on
Earth. Your ancestors were, at one time, all indigenous. Might we

regain a bit of our ancestors' indigeneity, much of which has likely been lost through time and travel? Your parents, grandparents, and great-grandparents who lived and breathed and experienced life before you—they are now living *through* you. From manifold generations back, they looked forward, sometimes even on their deathbeds, to your life. They and their indigeneity matter because you are here now, as their living hope.

Why does indigeneity matter? Because people who have lived on their own land from time immemorial have worked out their relationship with the plants, animals, weather, and mountains. Those relationships grew and matured over time until there were balance and harmony between the people indigenous to that place and the rest of the community of creation. In order to live in harmony and balance on the land, we all need to recover or discover truly Indigenous values.

We are all indigenous to some place. We are all from somewhere.

This is not to say we should all claim to be capital-*I* Indigenous. Most of us have settler ancestors: those who moved onto land not their own and displaced its original inhabitants. Others of us descend from people who did live somewhere in the world, for generations—people who once belonged to the land. We can all become more lowercase-*i* indigenous on the land. So perhaps we should all be asking the question, Who were we all before we were colonized or modernized or urbanized or westernized?

Like most people of nations composed of immigrant peoples, I am a finely crafted mix of various ethnic streams—and so, likely, are you. I was raised near Detroit, Michigan, and I am a Cherokee descendant recognized by the Keetoowah Band of Cherokee. This gives me no special rights or claims; it simply is. I have very little Indian ancestry, and as you will discover in this book, I was not raised much around Native American culture.

Although being Indian was a significant part of my identity growing up, I only began practicing a more traditionally oriented Indigenous lifestyle and way of thinking in my twenties. I have learned, over many years, to think differently than the dominant culture—the more I learned about an Indigenous way of viewing the world, the more natural it felt. I also realized that seeing all life as sacred and spiritual was what I had already learned while growing up: from my parents, grandparents, aunties, and uncles. I discovered that even though most of my family had been assimilated into Western society for generations, they still retained some Indigenous values. Perhaps the same is true for you.

Besides my limited Native American DNA, I also carry in my body the ancestry of numerous other nations from several continents. At one time, each of those peoples was indigenous to somewhere. They lived in a particular place, and they understood that distinct land and their place within it very well. Worldviews can be changed. Yes, true indigeneity is something earned over thousands of years. Yet if we try, we can all learn to adopt indigenous values into our lives—both from our own ancestry and, if we are very fortunate, from the Indigenous people who live *with* the land upon which we now live.

Planting your roots on the land in which you live is the only way to restore harmony and balance on Earth. The alternative is extremely bleak. If we fail to connect with the land in a very real and tangible way, we might still have a good life. But why miss out on the fullest of what life has to offer? Why miss out on learning from the greatest teacher, the Earth herself? Why miss seeing the beauty that awaits us in a renewed and fruitful relationship of mutual caring?

Becoming Rooted contains one hundred short meditations, or observances, to help us all become better Earth relatives. Like relatives, we are connected to one another whether we like it or not. The Earth and the whole community of creation live with us in a reciprocal relationship. What we do to the Earth and her creatures affects us. Without a strong relationship to the land, we will continue to flow with the dominant cultural view, objectifying the Earth and all her creatures: extracting, developing, and polluting without deep remorse. The Earth will not allow us to continue in this way. Even now, we are experiencing the "natural" disasters that could dominate our future.

I am inviting you on a one-hundred-day journey with creation. This journey will take you deeper into your own particular place—your own original somewhere. *Becoming Rooted* will help you encounter the particular place that makes you someone. The journey will help you get in touch with your own roots: with the land on which you now live and with the people who lived on that land for thousands of years prior to your arrival.

I hope you will allow these daily reflections, as seen through my particular Indigenous experience, to call you back to yours. I invite you not to mimic my experience but to integrate your own experiences, rooted in your sense of self and your own developing indigeneity. The book is for those recently indigenous to this land; Native Americans; and those who are many generations removed from their own indigeneity, which includes all immigrants. We all need to remember—or not forget in the first place—how to live with the Earth.

This journey is your personal invitation into a different kind of relationship with nature—or, as I like to say, with the whole community of creation. It is also an invitation into a different kind of relationship with Creator, however you understand Creator to be present in your own life and within everything—as God, as Great Mystery, as a higher power, or as the universe.

In these pages, I will intermix terms like *nature* and *creation*. I will talk about Creator, or Great Mystery, or God. As you read, feel free to substitute your own sense of the force you believe animates the universe. I come out of a Christian experience, so some of my references will be connected to that tradition. Your own spiritual or religious experience may be different from mine, be it Buddhism, Paganism, Daoism, Islam, Sikhism, or no formal religion whatsoever. Having taught world religions in graduate school for over a decade, I know that nearly every sacred tradition has within it an admiration for the natural world. The approach we will be taking on this journey goes deeper than any one religion. Our journey will embrace the commonality of our humanity as our spirituality. We are on this journey together.

We all have the Earth in common, no matter where we are from. Everyone in the whole community of creation has common cause to live well together on the Earth and to care for nature.

But please make no mistake: nature can be unforgiving. I have noticed that each of us feels a deep and primal longing both to experience nature and to protect ourselves from its harsh realities. This balance has been the plight of humanity for as long as we have inhabited the Earth. Despite our fear of the natural world, our fascination with the beauty of creation and her creatures—the whole community of creation, of which we are a part—never ceases.

On one hand, we wrap ourselves in the most concrete and blacktopped urban world imaginable. We cheer on the most philosophical of claims, the most rigorous of academic theories, and the most mechanistic of contraptions. On the other hand, a simple tree on the horizon, a hummingbird sipping its nectar, a rainbow, or freshly fallen snow still awakens our deepest sense of awe. In the process of protecting ourselves from the harshest realities in nature, we may not realize that most of the world has drifted far from our state of natural wonderment. Deep inside, though, often without realizing it, we miss nature's beauty and the sense of her inspiration.

Eloheh (pronounced "ay-luh-HAY") is a Cherokee word meaning "harmony," "wholeness," "abundance," "fullness," "peace," and much more. The vision for the nonprofit organization that my wife and I co-sustain came from a sacred and powerful dream I had in 1998. The results of that vision have come, after years of many joys and heartaches along the way. Located on ten acres, in the foothills of the Oregon Coastal Mountain Range, is the place we call home: *Eloheh Indigenous Center for Earth Justice and Eloheh Farm & Seeds*.

Our goal at Eloheh is to live in harmony with the land by using traditional Indigenous North American knowledge, wisdom, and practices as a guiding model that embodies educating our whole selves. At Eloheh my wife, Edith—who is an Eastern Shoshone tribal member—and I develop, implement, and teach sustainable and regenerative Earth practices. *Eloheh Farm* is a model of regenerative agriculture, animal husbandry, and wild-tending systems that support human needs while improving the land and all creation inhabiting the web of life here. We regularly hold schools, cohorts, and summits that teach these skills to others. More importantly, we hope to help others love the land on which they live.

To accept our place as simple human beings—beings who share a world with every seen and unseen creature in this vast community of creation—is to embrace our deepest spirituality. The journey we will take through these one hundred days will lead us away from the values and priorities of the "American dream"—or what I call an indigenous nightmare—toward a better understanding of what can be called "the harmony way." The harmony way is a universal set of values that I observed among many Indigenous peoples years prior to my PhD dissertation work, where I investigated the construct in a more in-depth way. The values within a harmony way framework have sustained many of the Indigenous people in the world over millennia. The values of the harmony way are the values that will sustain us well into the future.

We are all indigenous to some place. We are all from somewhere. We can all become rooted in the land that sustains us. I invite you on the journey.

PART ONE

LEARNING TO KNOW ALL OUR RELATIVES

1

PRACTICE SILENCE

Humankind has not woven the web of life. We are but one thread within it. Whatever we do to the web, we do to ourselves. All things are bound together. All things connect.
—Chief Seattle, Duwamish/Suquamish

I love the natural world, what I call *creation*. When I view the shimmering stars on a dark quiet night, or smell the deep forest of fallen leaves after a rain, or feel the sand slip through my feet as the salty ocean rolls over them, I feel at peace and at rest.

When I see the power of a lightning storm coming my way, or the approach of a curious black bear, or the too-close flight of an irritated wasp, I sense fear.

When I take in the grandeur of the ocean or Grand Canyon or Niagara Falls, my senses are overwhelmed with their beauty and their enormity.

And when I hear the babbling stream in a meadow with songbirds and crickets, I feel like they are making their presence known to me personally, and I feel loved.

All these experiences lead me naturally to better understand myself, others, and the Great Spirit. That Great Spirit—Creator, Great Mystery, or the universe, if you wish—has shared them all with me as gifts.

I will be the first to admit that I sometimes neglect creation. When I do that, I am rejecting the gifts of Creator. I still have much to learn. Like most Americans, I work and live a life full of distractions. But in my heart, I always long to be learning from Creator through the abundant gifts of nature in the most teachable place that I can find.

Some days it may only be watching a morning sunrise, or catching a glimpse of a hawk or deer while I'm driving, or listening to the wind. But I'm learning to savor those moments more than ever. Moments in which Great Spirit's silence can be heard in my heart. Moments in which Great Mystery's unspoken words can take root and grow—for a lifetime.

Sometimes the best answers are found in silence. Consider practicing listening in nature for an hour, several hours, or even a whole day.

2

SACRED FRACTALS

Long before I ever heard of Christ, or saw a White man, I learned from an untutored woman the essence of morality. With the help of dear nature herself, she taught me things simple but of mighty import. I knew God. I perceived what goodness is. I saw and loved what is really beautiful. Civilization has not taught me anything better.

—Ohiyesa (Charles Eastman), Dakota

A spring gently rises up out of the Earth and becomes a stream, which becomes a river, which becomes an ocean, which evaporates and becomes rain, which feeds itself back into the Earth again. Finding its way back to the surface, water repeats this sacred circle of enduring life.

Water, soil, seeds, plants, the sun, the stars, the moon: these are all our teachers. They teach us about life even as they give us life!

A fern is one of the best examples of enduring life. Scientists call the pattern of a fern a fractal. The natural world is full of fractals: patterns that repeat themselves at different scales. If you examine every part of the fern down to the smallest part of a leaf, you see it continuously repeating itself. I have read that a nautilus shell does something similar, but I have not seen one up close. In a way, everything has a bit of a fractal nature—repeating itself, giving new life, and moving itself forward into the future as a species.

We humans are beings of a fractal-type nature. We are born and we reproduce. Life, sacred life, continues naturally to our descendants. Like a stream, we are on an enduring journey to seek the sacredness of our lives as human beings. How well we choose to listen and how well we choose to live will determine how much of the sacredness we will discover.

Our most important teacher is dear nature: creation herself, Mother Earth. She holds the wisdom of the endless ages. If we can learn to cherish our beloved teacher and follow the wisdom found in her fractal-type patterns, we may survive the coming hardships.

Creation is continuously teaching us. Our human task is simply to look, and listen, and live well. She is teaching us now.

What patterns do you observe in the natural world? Look for patterns around you today.

3

SACRED SLEEP, SACRED WATER

And this our life, exempt from public haunt, finds tongues in trees, books in the running brooks, sermons in stones, and good in everything.

—William Shakespeare

When I was a teenager, growing up in the land of the Anishinabek, I had a secret spot. I would go there when I was hunting or just when I needed solace. About nine in the morning, when the warmth of the sun was winning the battle over the cold air left from the night before, I would make my way down to the creek where it exited the woods and joined a small field. The open space between two sections of woods was just wide enough to allow the heat from the sun to become a true force before the trees shadowed it out.

There I would lie, allowing the Earth to hold me in her warm embrace. I would close my eyes and listen to the gurgle of the creek. Those sacred moments often turned into calm sleep. That sleep was peaceful but not quiet.

Sleeping in the bosom of nature is not the same as sleeping in the safety of one's own home. Not at all. As you lay your body down to become one with the Earth, reality shifts. In that state, you can sense that God, Creator, is listening to the intentions of your heart. Whatever the mysterious power is behind creation, it softens one's mind. Great Mystery unscrews the tight lids of the jars of certainty that you hold too tightly, too fiercely. You realize, sometimes even trembling, that something greater than yourself is meeting you.

There, in the restful unknown world between sleep and wakefulness, you give yourself to those elements, to Spirit, in the kind of vulnerability a newborn to the world must experience.

As I dozed off into the realm of sacred beauty next to that stream, I listened to how the water responded to each rock, to every branch protruding from the creek bank, and to the swirl of every curve as it meandered past me and into some other creature's nap. With each contact, the water had a particular note and registry of sound.

Over the rocks, around the curve, and down the path of its sacred water journey. Sacred sleep. Sacred water. Sacred life.

Who listened to the land before your people group arrived? How do you imagine their sacred moments?

4

WHAT THE PLANT PEOPLE ARE SAYING

Life is a series of natural and spontaneous changes. Don't resist them; that only creates sorrow. Let reality be reality. Let things flow naturally forward in whatever way they like.

—Lao Tzu

Change is difficult. Some things change naturally over time: the course of a river, the shore of an ocean, the direction a tree decides to grow. Other changes are artificial. When humans interfere with the course of nature in an unnatural way—such as by damming a river—we are bound to experience unknown and often unwanted consequences.

Humanity has yet to realize the fact that nature is wiser and more powerful than we are. Nature will, without a doubt, outlive us. She knows her mind, and she understands what keeps life in balance. Today we seldom see nature in her unmolested glory, so we rarely consider the degree to which human civilization has changed what is natural to what is unnatural.

I have heard from elders in the past few years that our medicine plants are not nearly as potent as they used to be. They say the Earth is weakening; an unnatural change has occurred. The plant people, as we call them, have become nutrient deficient, and weaker. Modern Western science has come to the same realization by explaining that as more carbon is released into the atmosphere, plants are less able to develop the nutrients needed. What modern science tells us about creation is what our Indigenous elders have been observing for millennia.

Now more than ever, we need people with keen observational skills to help us recover and retain the truth in nature. Indigenous wisdom has had a long relationship with creation, based on an ethic of harmony and respect. Modern scientific methods often confirm the simplest truths that our Indigenous teachers have always known. It's really quite simple. Science verifies what scientists observe. In more than one sense, our Indigenous elders have always been scientifically aware. Western scientists use tools that tell them the hydrological cycles have changed. Our elders know the huckleberries are ripening a month later than usual. Both observe verifiable knowledge. One is abstract while the other is very personal. As each plant, insect, animal, or bird moves closer to extinction, the unnatural changes in our world become immeasurable.

What we can agree upon is that the Earth has been changed, unnaturally. No matter whether we consult science or Indigenous wisdom, together we can affirm that it is not a good change.

How have you noticed the Earth changing? Can you do just one thing each day to help restore nature to her former glory?

5

THE EARTH'S SKIN

Everything is possessed of personality, only different from us in form. Knowledge is inherent in all things. The world is a library, and its books are the stones, leaves, grass, brooks, and the birds and animals that share, alike with us, the storms and blessings of earth.

—Luther Standing Bear, Lakota

My wife and I are, among other things, planter farmers. To us, few things smell or feel better than cool, dark, rich, moist, worm-filled dirt. We realized at some point that keeping the soil healthy is perhaps our most important obligation. Edith and I have found a number of natural ways to create healthy soil through planting well, creating worm beds, and composting.

Topsoil is the Earth's skin. Our own skin protects the rest of our body from infection. If we poison it or cut it or burn it, we suffer. Our Indigenous people have always believed the Earth is alive and all things are interconnected. The Earth, as a living entity, has always been something we took for granted. But it's actually a miracle. Thanks to the power of microscopes, we discovered that the Earth is alive and interconnected in many unique ways. There are sacred, invisible communities that live in healthy soil. In just one cup of healthy, undisturbed soil live two hundred billion bacteria, twenty million protozoa, one hundred thousand meters of fungi, fifty thousand arthropods, and one hundred thousand nematodes. This reality, though microscopic, is almost beyond our imagination!

Given the scope of things, Edith and I have had to concede that we are not the real farmers on our farm. The real farmers are the invisible communities of microorganisms who actually do most of the work. Our job is simply to keep them healthy by using organic and safe liquids in our home, never using poisons or other toxic sprays, and utilizing natural and organic farming methods.

Our duty is to think about how each thing we do affects the rest of the community of creation—even its smallest members who keep the Earth's skin healthy.

What vow could you make to protect the Earth's skin? Or what small thing could you do today to keep it healthy?

6

THE ELK AND THE LOON

God is the friend of silence. See how nature—trees, flowers, grass—grows in silence; see the stars, the moon and the sun, how they move in silence. We need silence to be able to touch our souls.

—Mother Teresa

There remain very few places on the Earth where one can go to experience silence. Often when we try to escape into nature, our bliss is interrupted by the distant sounds of tires hugging the road, or airplanes flying overhead, or even dirt bikes driving by (which I have a particular aversion to—sorry, dirt-bikers).

Many meditative practices rely on a semblance of silence that, through discipline, drowns out the noise of the world. Still, sound is ever present. When escaping to more remote places, I have taught myself to ignore the unwanted sounds and embrace those that feed my spirit. Two sounds never fail to connect me to my deepest primordial spirit-heart.

One is that of an elk bugle. During my years in Colorado, I would go archery hunting for elk. (I should state up front that I never actually killed an elk.) Archery hunters must find a way to draw the bull elk close. That means having only about fifty yards between yourself and a huge, excited, seven-hundred-pound wild creature with large antlers that can take down bushes and small trees at will.

My advantage was that I could imitate the elk's bugle. Every fall for several years, I looked forward to calling elk. It became an annual pleasure. In fact, I was never disappointed by not getting one as long as I had a good calling session. The elk's "bugle" is more of a whistle when it begins; it then transitions to a howl and finally a grunt. In this sound is found the elk's deepest urge to challenge everything around him so his lineage may remain on Earth. Somehow, there is an echo there within my own soul.

The other sound that reconnects me to sacred Earth—actually my favorite sound in the world—is that of a loon. The loon's call resonates deep within my very being. I have no words to explain it but to say that it both excites me and gives me deep peace. The loon's call is both mystery and beauty, primordial and addictive, and I long for it always.

I love to experience other sounds as well: the sweet song of a cardinal, the cooing of a mourning dove, the simple rush of ocean waves. These are the true songs of my heart that let me know that I am connected to the whole community of creation.

What sounds in nature speak to your soul? If you know, can you seek them more often? If you're not sure, what could you do to discover them?

7

NATURE SPEAKING

Just ask the animals, and they will teach you. Ask the birds of the sky, and they will tell you. Speak to the earth, and it will instruct you. Let the fish in the sea speak to you.

—Job 12:7–8

My ancestral DNA apparently gave me an inclination toward single-mindedness. When my mind is set on one thing, I am rarely distracted. On one occasion, after I had spoken to a crowd, a woman came up to me afterward and apologized profusely that her young child had crawled around the lectern and at my feet during my presentation. I hadn't even noticed.

My wife has learned that if she doesn't pull my attention from whatever I am currently doing or even thinking about, her words simply become background noise. Edith often hears the same refrain from me: "Honey, what were you saying?"

Nature is always speaking, but we are not often listening. I don't expect my wife to remain silent just because I am in deep thought. It's up to me to listen to her—to acknowledge her and to pay attention to what she is telling me. Would you ask your loved ones not to make their needs known? To keep silent instead of holding a conversation?

We are in a relationship with the Earth and with all of Earth's creatures. We must amplify the Earth's voice. We must protect it by recognizing the Earth's rights.

Unfortunately, we have waited until this late hour to realize the sacredness of this relationship. Let's not delay until it is too late.

Talk to animals and then be taught by them. Talk to and listen to birds. Talk to the Earth and other parts of creation and expect to be taught from them. Listen to fish attest to the truth. And recognize Creator's hand in all creation.

Support and volunteer for a nonprofit that works to preserve and amplify the Earth's voice.

8

THE HARMONY WAY

On reading the various accounts . . . by explorers and anthropologists, what strikes one is the almost universal hospitality shown by Indian tribes, especially to their White visitors. . . . There are practically no examples of inhospitality or harsh treatment rendered to Whites. On the contrary, the tribal leaders went out of their way to receive these visitors as special guests.
—Carl Starkloff

The harmony way is a way of living that undergirds all of Native American history, religion, traditions, ceremonies, stories, philosophy, and relationships. Referred to by different names among the various tribal nations, the harmony way is planted firmly within an Indigenous worldview. According to a set of values that are interconnected, the way of harmony and balance encompasses both being and doing and is applied to all of life. The harmony way is a meaningful whole.

Harmonious and reconciled relations with others result when a deep respect characterizes those relationships. The wisdom of Indigenous traditions and stories emphasizes the importance of restoring the relationships that exist among Creator, humans, animals, and the Earth—what I call the community of creation. One of the principle values found within the way of harmony is generosity, often expressed through hospitality. Other values include respect for everything and a lifestyle of gratitude, especially to the Earth, which produces well and in abundance.

A society with harmony-way values cares for the most marginalized—for the poor and needy—because how we treat those who are most in need reveals the heart of who we are. Such a society will protect Mother Earth, our source of life, at every turn.

The harmony way is meant to be both personal (emphasizing our relationships with other beings) and structural (replacing unjust systems where harmony has been broken). To create a society based on the harmony way means the old structures and systems will need to be replaced with new structures and systems.

The expectation for all creation to live in harmony has been developed by America's Indigenous peoples over thousands of years. Harmony is the way of nature and, by design, the way of Creator. Creator expects us to reshape the world we know into the world intended for all creation to live well together.

Today, both people and nature have great needs. What can you do today to extend hospitality to the community of creation on a personal or a structural level?

9

TO ALL MY RELATIVES

A translation of mitakuye oyasin would better read: "For all the above me and below me and around me things." That is, for all my relations . . . it is this understanding of inter-relatedness, of balance and mutual respect of the different species in the world, that characterizes what we might call Indian people's greatest gift to Amer-Europeans and to the Amer-European understanding of creation at this time of world ecological crisis.

—Clara Sue Kidwell, Homer Noley, and George E. Tinker

In Lakota, *mitakuye oyasin* means something like "for all the above me and below me and around me things." In Cherokee, it is *hi-da-da-tse-li.* Once I asked a Navajo friend, "What is *Sá'ąh Naagháí Bik'eh Hózhóón*?" His reply: "I don't know; it's just our life, the way we live in harmony and beauty."

I think most Indigenous peoples have some word for or understanding of this way of being—a way that sees us as living in deep relationship with other humans and all species. I suspect all human beings desire to live according to what I sometimes call "the original instructions." Perhaps it's similar to what some call "the common good." Indigenous people understand this way of living as not a future utopia but simply the way to be now.

By giving credence to the idea that all people are related to each other, we open ourselves to the possibility of once again becoming family with all humanity. By realizing the connectedness of humankind to all animal life and life in every form, we become aware of new possibilities for learning and becoming active in species preservation. By studying humanity's dependence upon creation, we learn how to sustain our planet, and we learn fresh prospects for developing food, water, and renewable energy.

What if we are all related? What if the Lakota prayer—for all that is above me, and all that is below me, and everything that is around me—is a prayer said on behalf of our relatives?

Most important of all, every human creature could realize the fact that peace is attainable if we are all willing to say, "We are all related."

Stand outside and look around you. Name some of the relatives you have neglected.

10

A POWERFUL DREAM

With one mind, we turn to honor and thank all the Food Plants we harvest from the garden. Since the beginning of time, the grains, vegetables, beans, and berries have helped the people survive. Many other living things draw strength from them, too. We gather all the Plant Foods together as one and send them a greeting of thanks.

—From the Haudenosaunee Thanksgiving Prayer

My wife and I were returning from a speaking engagement in New Mexico where we had been engaged in sharing along with other Indigenous spiritual leaders and elders. We had had a very good trip and had learned much from the wisdom of others. We ended up having to leave the gathering early, however; at eight thousand feet, the altitude just became too much for my asthma.

On the way home, I had a dream. It was the most profound dream of my life.

My mantra back then was "We are healing the land." I'm pretty sure I said it at that gathering, probably several times. We had already begun living out our big vision, which would eventually become *Eloheh Indigenous Center for Earth Justice and Eloheh Farm & Seeds*. On that land we had schools, and ceremony, and the constant extension of hospitality. We understood the great need to restore the land to health through regenerative land practices and farming. We cared deeply about the land, including every tree and bush we planted and every one that was there when we arrived. We were healing the land Creator gave us, right?

The night before we arrived home, I had the dream that changed my perspective. I'd had profound dreams in the past, in which animals spoke to me. But in this dream, all the plants at Eloheh Farm—both those considered wild and those considered domestic—stood in front of me. The dream was simple and pure in its essence: just me standing in front of all the plants, as if I needed to answer to them for something. With one singular voice, they said, "*We* are healing *you*!"

The message was absolutely primordial in nature and equally as humbling. I was dumbstruck the whole day after the dream, living in a contemplative state between embarrassment and true humility. They, the plants, were healing me.

I felt a sense of my brevity on this Earth compared to the oaks and other trees surrounding me—trees who had been here long before I was born and would be here long after I die. Every medicine plant, food plant, shelter plant, beauty plant, and others—these are our helper friends.

Later that day, we stopped at the Redwood Forest in Northern California. So much oxygen filled my entire mind and body that I felt like I had been holding my breath for years. The words came back to me: "*We* are healing *you*."

Take time today to speak to the many helper plants that surround you. Discover and give thanks to each one for how they contribute to your life.

PART TWO

CELEBRATING THE COMMUNITY OF CREATION

11

NATURAL GROWTH

In nature, nothing is perfect and everything is perfect. Trees
can be contorted, bent in weird ways, and they're still beautiful.
—Alice Walker

Everything in creation is designed to survive. We are created to
reach out into the future and reassure our progeny that they will
make it in the world. Plants and trees know where to place their
branches and leaves in order to receive the needed sun. Their leaves
are designed to drink falling rain and direct it to drip where the
roots are growing. As the excess water drains down the stem, it slips
down to the thick base of the plant. Plant blossoms are designed by
color, shape, and timing to lure just the right pollinators in order
to assure their future.

Without the help of microscopic bacteria, minerals, and fungi,
plants won't grow. Without the right pollinators, most plants
can't reproduce themselves. Unless they receive the water needed,
healthy plants languish and die. Birds also help the plants by
eating their seeds, and their droppings expand that plant's territory. Squirrels and other rodents do the same for trees. Rain, soil,

bacteria, fungus, minerals, bees and other insects, birds, squirrels, and a whole host of other creatures we know about—and likely those we don't—are all vital to the survival of our shared creation.

We all need help. We are all designed to be part of a greater community, more than just ourselves. We are all a part of the community of creation.

If we are to survive the future, we must consider our helpers and how we can help to sustain them. As human beings, we have the privilege to choose to be co-sustainers. What does it take to have healthy flora and fauna on Mother Earth? What about the health of nature in our communities? Our neighborhoods and even our own backyards all need our support. Have we cut off parts of the natural community or impeded their growth? What are the roadblocks that prevent nature from expressing growth around us?

Our relationships with all our nonhuman friends are reciprocal. We need their support as much as they need ours. We are all one big family working together for health and growth and well-being. We are all related.

What one thing can you do to take down an impediment to nature's growth? Or how could you add a pathway of some kind so nature can do what nature naturally wants to do: grow?

12

NATURAL REMINDERS

When the student is ready, the teacher will appear.

—Mr. Miyagi

I once had the privilege of spending a few days with a particular Cherokee elder and spiritual leader. I had inherited one of his ceremonies through someone he had mentored who had taught it to me. I wanted to be sure to glean as much instruction and wisdom from him as I could during these rare few days together.

He was not as tall as I had imagined, but that didn't diminish his natural authority. He was somewhat wrinkled, like most men in their late seventies or early eighties, although I didn't ask his age. As I listened to his thick Oklahoma Cherokee accent, one unique to those whose first language is not English, I heard a wisdom born of time and experience. His speech was unhurried. He was measured, deliberate, sedate, and dignified. I could sense I was in the presence of a man who not only knew much about the natural world but understood it.

I will never forget what he said about a spider. "When you see a spider in your house, don't kill it!" he said. "Go get a tissue or something and gently pick it up and set it outside. Tell it, 'Spider, you are welcome to live here, just not in the house. So don't come back in.'" As I considered that simple instruction, I decided that kindness shown to a spider is important. But his admonition was also a lesson about building character, about our capacity to live well *with* the community of creation, not lord over it. The elder understood that smashing spiders may lead a person down one path and that saving spiders may lead down another.

I have kept up the practice of saving spiders and other bugs, as much as possible, throughout the years. Many years later, I was sitting in a large talking circle at Hopiland in Arizona. As someone else was sharing, I got a text message that said the elder in this story had passed over the previous night. I felt sad and contemplative at the same time. What a tragic loss to the world when any one of our wise elders passes.

While deep in thought about his passing, I noticed that, walking across the wide-open space in the circle, was a large spider. Someone across the room noticed too, and he stood up to stomp the spider. "Wait," I said. Everyone in the circle quietly watched as I went to the restroom for some toilet paper and walked up slowly to the spider. As I escorted it to the door, they heard me say, "Spider, you are welcome here, but not inside. Now don't come back."

The circle—from the elder, to me, to others—was complete. Now spoken into another circle, the reminder began again.

Be kind to spiders and other creatures, especially the ones you don't naturally favor. Remind yourself to treat them well—for your sake, for their sake, and for others to observe.

13

CORN

Selu stood over a large cane basket and then opened her vest, scraping her fingernails on her ribs, underneath her breasts, and corn began to flow from her body into the basket. . . . And she said to her sons, before you kill me, promise me you will cut my body into thirteen pieces and drag them over all parts of Cherokee country. The two boys did as she asked and corn began to grow everywhere.

—Traditional Cherokee Story

I consider myself a son of Selu and Kanati, the first woman and man in Cherokee mythology. I know I am a son of Selu (pronounced "SHAY-loo") because I grow corn every year. By doing so, I stay connected to our story. Each corn seed I harvest is valuable to me, as if it were a precious jewel. Each corn seed is loved by me. When I hold them in my hand, I feel a sense of abundance.

What I feel when holding *selu*, my corn-mother, is more than a feeling of accomplishment that the Earth has once again favored my corn seed and nature has once again granted me a harvest. In a sense, these seeds speak to me—of my lineage, my heritage, my wealth, and my future. The corn seed gives me my identity.

Because I no longer live in Cherokee country, I don't get much opportunity to participate in our ceremonies, most of which involve corn. But I try to do what I can by marking the calendar and remembering the ceremonies in some tangible way. Some ceremonies I celebrate elaborately; blessing the seeds and planting, for example, become a great ordeal as a result. Other ceremonies I simply imagine and remember. Sometimes my limitations—being so remote from the origins of these ceremonies—remind me of my truncated experience. Some varieties of my Cherokee corn, for example, only grow to be ten to twelve feet tall here in Oregon, whereas in Cherokee country, they usually grow to be fourteen or fifteen feet tall! I apologize to the corn for the fact that I am not planting it in Cherokee soil. We all do the best we can.

Growing corn and remembering its importance—and calling it by its proper Cherokee name, *selu*—connects me to my ancestors. And yes, I also love to eat corn. Corn can be made into flour or meal that can, in turn, be made into cornbread. Corn, treated in a specific way, turns into hominy. I love simple corn on the cob, fried corn, and dried corn stew, and I have many other favorites like corn chowder, popcorn, and corn pudding.

Through her sacrifice, Selu has given us much to enjoy! When I gently hold the corn seed in my hands, it helps me remember who I am.

What foods come from your own heritage? What celebrations included that food? What can you do to continue that tradition?

14

TOGETHER

When one tugs at a single thing in nature, he finds it attached to the rest of the world.

—John Muir

There is nothing singular in the whole of creation. From the widest view of the multiverse to the most subatomic level, nothing exists alone. Everything relies on something else. When you break down an atom into its fundamental parts, even within those parts are things called quarks, which move around but are always found with others.

A simple flower or tree may look alone in a field, but it, too, is part of the community of creation. Plants are eaten or used for medicine or for some sort of shelter. Flowers need to be pollinated by bees and other insects and even by the wind. Insects like bees produce honey, which feeds their young, and we enjoy it as well. Honey gives us nutrition and endorphins that improve our state of mind. Our happiness spreads to others. One system after another relates to another system, which affects all creation. Nothing exists to be alone.

Some parts of creation appear to be solitary. Of all the blue herons I've seen in my life, only once have I seen two spending much time together. But blue herons do eventually "get together." Sea turtles stay out to sea for many years at a time. During this time, they travel alone—but then, as if by some magic, they all come together at once.

People are the same way. Some of us are loners, and some of us are very social. But even the loners seem to need company at some point. As my grandma used to say at the end of each of our visits, "I like comers, and I like goers."

The universe is a system of sacred circles, all related to one another. All needing each other. We are never alone.

Take notice today of something you see or do, and consider the connection it has to something else. See yourself in the circle.

15

DIVERSITY

Our ability to reach unity in diversity will be the beauty and test of our civilization.

—Mahatma Gandhi

No two fingerprints are exactly alike. No retinal patterns are a perfect match. Our voices differ enough to allow voice recognition software to work. Even among identical twins, there is a world of difference.

I could examine a thousand sparrows and not be able to see the differences between them. But the differences are there; each one is different from the others. Each snowflake is different from the others. Each molecule on the planet seems different from the next.

Homogeneity, or sameness, is an illusion that can at times give us comfort. We like to be around people like us. When we are around people like ourselves, we feel like we can relax, or we feel safe. Perhaps this sense of tribalism is a primal instinct carried forth in our DNA. Our relationship to sameness is, if anything, natural.

Yet when we examine anyone else very closely, we find worlds of difference. I can first look at someone and think they are similar to me—but then I discover that we're very different. It's like how each bird of a flock of a thousand sparrows is different. The sense of superficial sameness allows us short-term comfort, but it never lasts. Once we really get to know a person, we either learn to appreciate and even embrace the differences, or we avoid and even reject the differences. Embracing difference builds both character and community.

Everything in the universe is different because we are not made only to live in comfort and the security of superficial sameness. We were also made to explore and learn from the differences.

Try to put yourself in a situation where you are different from those around you. It can be uncomfortable at first, but encountering differences allows you to work on your curiosity and your character.

16

HUMAN-CENTERED

Regardless of whether or not they have roots or fins or legs or wings, they are all my relatives.

—Winona LaDuke

Anthropocentrism is a fancy word to describe the view that humans are above nature. An anthropocentric worldview understands humanity as having the right of supreme rule over all creation—to the point that all creation is subject to human desires. An anthropocentric worldview allows human beings to view the resources of the world as commodities made for human pleasure or extraction without thought of the whole of the ecosystemic reality. An anthropocentric worldview does not see the intimate relationship we share with all creation in the web of life.

In *The Song of Trees,* biologist George David Haskell gives an example of a different way of viewing the relationship between humans and other beings in the natural world. When asked to describe specific trees by their general type, the Waorani people in the Amazon rainforest could not do it. In order to describe a tree, the Waorani found it necessary to also describe the tree's ecological context. In the minds of the Waorani, like many Indigenous peoples, the tree does not stand alone in creation. Each tree, like every other creature, exists in relationship to its surroundings.

We are all intricately linked to all of creation. We are related to the world around us. What if we began to see other creatures as necessary and as family? In the words of Indigenous activist and planter Winona LaDuke, "They are all our relatives."

When you look at a tree, do you see only that tree? Or do you see the forest, the soil, the birds, the animals, the air, and the humanity connected to it? If you see only the tree, chances are it will become an object to you. If you see the tree as a part of a family, it becomes your relative.

Observe a tree today in its context of the whole community of creation. How is it related to the other living things around it? How is it related to you?

17

WATER, SACRED TO US ALL

When the well's dry, we know the worth of water.
—Benjamin Franklin

For several years, we packed up our kids and a few belongings in an old van and traveled from one Indian reservation to another as we served Indigenous people in a variety of ways. On our trips, we learned in new ways the way that water is sacred to America's Indigenous people. Water is sacred to us all.

One year, we were honored to be present for a blessing ceremony on the Big Grassy Reserve in Ontario, Canada. In the early spring, the Ojibwe community blesses the lake. They say prayers, sing songs, and speak words to reestablish any lost connection in that great circle of life, which includes the people and the fish and the lake.

Across Turtle Island is Hopiland. In the Bean Dance, as with most ceremonies among the peoples of the Southwest, the Hopi nation prays for rain. And I think that's about all the Hopi would like said about that. With deep gratitude to the Hopi, we were their guests for the Bean Dance.

Traditionally, Cherokee people do a going-to-water ceremony, during which songs are sung in the morning to greet the day at the creek or river's edge or next to a spring. These ceremonies continue to this day. I am among those who continue to practice the Cherokee water ceremony, if even in a small way.

Among the Pacific Northwest nations of Indigenous peoples, borders disappear during their annual Canoe Journey. Canoe Journey is a chance for those various tribal peoples to reestablish themselves once again. The Pacific Ocean, with its bays and inlets and beaches, has provided so much for the people over millennia.

You have a daily relationship with water. Perhaps we all can agree on a few simple truths:

- Our aquifers are being overpumped well beyond their recharge rates.
- Rising temperatures are boosting evaporation rates.
- Rainfall patterns are now severely altered, and inadequate snowmelts are not properly feeding rivers and streams in the dry season.
- Water tables are falling, with whole lakes now disappearing.
- Glaciers are melting at alarming rates. The tundra is melting.
- Water shortages translate to food shortages.
- Global water consumption doubles about every twenty years. The UN expects demand to outstrip supply by 30 percent in 2040.
- Global corporate opportunists, who see the absolute devastation coming, are attempting to buy up the world's water supplies for profit.

Water is sacred. No one can live without water.

Savor water enough to save it for everyone. Today, try to use less water as you wash, cook, or clean. Become active politically on behalf of water.

18

MEMORIES OF WATER

We forget that the water cycle and the life cycle are one.

—Jacques Cousteau

I have many fond memories of water as a child. My first significant water memory is of a simple well at my grandparents' farm in Mississippi. I remember watching my older siblings crank up the water—I was still too young to do so, they said. When I was a preteen, the first challenge was earning the right to retrieve drinking water for the home from my grandfather, who we called "Papaw." The second challenge was actually cranking the water-filled bucket all the way back up without spilling it.

Cranking it down was the fun part, but cranking it smoothly so as to not spill half the bucket on the way back up? That was work. I was determined to do it myself, without asking one of my older siblings or cousins for help. The reward—besides an accepting smile from my grandfather—was the first drink out of the bucket. On sweltering hot Mississippi days in July, that pure, cold water was a treat well worth the effort to retrieve it!

On that same farm, a creek afforded us grandchildren both a playground and a place to catch minnows and crawdads that the older grandkids could use for bait. The creek ran into the pond, where we could fish. My earliest memories of that pond were of my Papaw teaching me to fish there. Fishing included a twelve-foot cane pole with a fishing line tied on the end; on the other end of the line was a bobber and a hook. We always visited the chicken yard with our flashlights the night before, turning over pieces of wood and other debris to find wiggly night crawlers. Into the can of dirt they went, to be called on the next morning for their sacred duty.

That often mirror-still pond wasn't large, but it held untold hidden treasures. Lurking below the surface of that still pond lay catfish, bass, and bluegill—sunfish, to be exact. I learned there that catching fish meant we would eat fish for lunch or supper that day. The water supplied our food. The water provided our enjoyment. The water gave us memories of family and the importance of the circle of life.

The worms, the fish, my grandfather, the meals, the creek, the pond, the rain, me—it was all part of the sacred circle. Sometimes I long for some undisturbed time to fish in that pond again, with just a cane pole, a string, a bobber, and a hook.

What are your favorite water memories? Share them with someone today. Consider making a water memory for any young ones in your life.

19

MAKING ROOM

Heaven is under our feet as well as over our heads.
—Henry David Thoreau

Edith and I have started and sustained three farms together. One was fifty acres, one was almost four acres, and our current farm is just under ten acres. In each of these places, wildlife was abundant if you had an eye to see it.

Although we were farming, we always made room for the non-farm creatures. Even on the smallest farm, we set aside a half acre that was theirs, not ours. That little half acre had a creek running through it. Growing on it were snowberries, which are food for the birds but poisonous to humans; rose hips; blackberries; and all sorts of diverse trees, grasses, and plants.

We tried to create an unmolested home for the birds and animals and all the creatures we couldn't see. We were rewarded often by seeing red-tailed hawks, woodpeckers, blue herons, songbirds, rabbits, squirrels, deer, skunks, and even a visiting coyote every so often.

Sure, we could have used that half acre for something else. We could have planted corn and other crops, or cut down the trees for firewood, or simply used it for wild-tending indigenous plants.

But we had to ask ourselves, How much is enough? How much land do we really need to make it, and is it ever worth driving all the wildlife away? They need space too. If we would have used that space for our own needs, our community would be the poorer for it.

Take a look around your own yard, neighborhood, and community. See the potential for plants, trees, and other wildlife. Give them some space.

20

SAME THING TWICE

Our life is an apprenticeship to the truth, that around every circle another can be drawn; that there is no end in nature, but every end is a beginning; that there is always another dawn risen. . . . There are no fixtures in nature.

—Ralph Waldo Emerson

Every night, Edith and I look out our back windows to see the sunset on the Coastal Mountain Range of Oregon. This has become something of a ritual for us. The sunsets change colors each night, as does the area of sky affected by the various shades of usually orange light. Once in a while, there are no clouds present, and sometimes the fog obscures a clear view. Often the clouds give us a different picture each day as the sun sets.

Sometimes the clouds on the mountains are puffy and huge. At other times, they are long and thin. My favorite is when the long clouds rest just below the horizon and we can still see the tops of the mountain. On those evenings, the clouds make the mountains look mysterious and even eerie.

Each evening, the sun—because of the Earth's rotation—sets in a slightly different place on the mountains. It gives off different shades of brightness—sometimes bright and blinding, sometimes sullen and lulling. So far, we have watched a different sunset each night. It's never the same thing twice.

I remind myself that the sun sets in different places around the world, not just over our mountains. Every person, bird, and animal is looking at the same sunset from a different angle. We all see the same thing, but we see it differently. This is the beauty of life.

I even wonder sometimes, Are Edith and I, looking out the same window, seeing the same sunset? It helps to see life from the perspective of others. Left only to our own views, we might miss much of the beauty and intrigue life has to offer. What I see from my vantage point, you may not see. What you see may be slightly, or even very, different than my singular view.

Life is like that. Each member of the community of creation partakes in it, and each views it from their own place. Sunsets continue throughout all our lives, having important lessons for us all. Each lesson is valuable, but none are the same.

Consider the views of others today. What might a sunset—or an issue, or a story, or an idea—look like if you were standing where they do?

PART THREE

ACCEPTING THE INVITATION TO AN INDIGENOUS WORLDVIEW

21

WE ARE STILL HERE

Generations come and generations go, but the earth never changes. The sun rises and the sun sets, then hurries around to rise again. The wind blows south, and then turns north. Around and around it goes, blowing in circles. Rivers run into the sea, but the sea is never full. Then the water returns again to the rivers and flows out again to the sea.

—Ecclesiastes 1:4–7

Throughout Indian country, one phrase rings true. No matter where you go, "We are still here!"

We are still here. It may not seem like such a profound statement. At first, anyway. But given the numerous attempts at cultural assimilation and genocide that have decimated many Native American populations by 95 percent since 1492—and given that Indigenous people still have some of the worst living conditions on Turtle Island—the statement means a lot. "We are still here" speaks directly to the hope that remains in America's First Nations.

In Indian country, any hope is good hope. This hope—sustained through poverty, racism, poor housing, chronic disease, and a host of other maladies—is not based on utopianism. The earned hope of which I speak is built on a spirituality of relationship with the land and with all living creation and on respect for elders who sacrificed to give the generations to follow them a future. In that sense, maybe a better way to honor the sacrifices of those who came before is to say, "We are still here because they were here before us."

This very real hope recognizes that Earth endures and that we can still do enough to reverse the damage done. After all, the Earth is much stronger and more resilient than any human being. Although human beings are a part of the Earth, we may be the most expendable. This gives me pause—as well as a much longer view of our history and our future.

I think Mother Earth is going to be OK in the end. I just hope we will be here long enough to see it. Although it might make us feel pretty insignificant, another way to turn the phrase is this: "We are still here . . . for now. But the Earth remains forever."

On what foundation is your hope secured? List the certainties in your life if everything else (home, land, family, religion, means of making a living) were taken away.

22

LISTENING AND UNDERSTANDING

The renowned reporter Dan Rather once asked Mother Teresa what she says to God when she prays. "I listen," she replied. Somewhat startled, Mr. Rather then asked her, "What does God say to you when you listen?" Without pause or change of expression on her face, Mother Teresa simply said, "He listens."

Indigenous people who are raised traditionally are taught to listen in every situation. Like most values, this skill is caught more than taught. Generations of people living close to the Earth learn that listening skills are vital. When hunting, for example, it's not just visual observations that matter but also one's listening skills.

I was not raised traditionally. Several generations of assimilating to the dominant cultural worldview mostly separated me from such values. Yet somehow they made their way into my life despite the pressure from Western acculturation. I spent countless hours as a child—and later as an adult—alone, listening to what nature had to say.

I understand that a shallow place in the river makes a certain kind of bubbling sound and that it is much louder than the sleepy, serene sound of a deeper spot in the river. I can tell a bull elk call from a cow elk grunt from the bark of the leader cow warning the herd to beware. I understand when the wind is trying to tell me a change of weather is coming soon. Still, all in all, I think my understandings are very limited.

A Machupta/Maidu tribal elder once told me how to listen to the sound of birds while looking for herbal medicines in the woods. The particular sound of the birds associated with each plant, he said, would lead me to the medicine I was seeking. I listened to my friend's words. He gave a number of examples. Unfortunately, I did not follow through with the practice. So sadly, to this day, I have little understanding of birdsong and the medicine plants with which they are associated.

Those who live in a culture that values oral tradition and the natural world will learn to be good listeners. Listening is the first lesson of knowing. But only lived experience creates understanding.

Listening to the natural world doesn't necessarily lead to understanding it, but it's a start. What type of listening practice can you implement today?

23
PLACE

People are trapped in history and history is trapped in them.
—James Baldwin

Place is everything. We relate to either a real place or an abstract sense of place. The Western world creates a category of place and then universalizes it, making it abstract. When Great Mystery made this world, it was designed to be a place for relationship among Creator, human beings, and all of creation. Each part is related to the other, and each is different in its role. All are equally important.

Each place contains a rich geographic and sociocultural history. That history—which includes the host people of that land and all creatures who inhabit it—makes a particular environment. Each place consists of particular water features, elevations, flora and fauna, insects, and soil. Every place is unique.

To universalize a place is to neglect our human purpose. When we depersonalize a place, we begin to abuse the land. Ignoring the history of a place or treating it superficially shows extreme hubris. To treat one species in that particular environment as more important than the others displays arrogance, and we do so at our own peril.

It is common for Indigenous peoples to understand one specific place. As a result, they understand their relationship to that particular place. The context of that relationality, as it relates to place, exists in Indigenous people's own stories and revelations. Their relationship to that place is embodied in ceremonies and in food practices. They know its weather patterns and its landscape. Each particular Indigenous group understands its own land.

Hundreds of generations have lived with the land on which you live. What values can you learn from the tribal group who understands that land?

24

THE CIRCLE

We inter-breathe with the rain forests, we drink from the oceans. They are part of our own body.

—Thich Nhat Hanh

One model of understanding our relationship to everything is a simple symbol used among Native Americans: the circle. The harmony way of living is often referred to symbolically as a circle or a hoop. Among Native Americans, the harmony way is less like a philosophy and more like a whole way of being and doing life.

To European and Western people, a philosophy is something that one can adopt at any point in life. A philosophy can simply be believed or espoused. But the harmony way is a way of living and being, with very tangible expressions. Living out the harmony way requires not just a belief but also actions that align with and participate in the local ecosystem and the whole universe. The circle is the tangible symbol that represents this understanding.

Perhaps you remember when you were a child and an adult said something like "OK, kids, gather around," or "Let's get in a circle," or simply, "Circle up." Circles are found in nature; perhaps that's why we are so comfortable imitating the pattern. A circle seems like the natural way to gather together, each person able to see the eyes of everyone else. Each hand clasped to the person next to themselves. Each body, creating an impenetrable ring of protection. A circle is a very natural and comfortable way to come together.

The circle has no beginning and no end, so one can enter at any place or stage. The circle can explain stages of life, values, and different people groups. Circles can explain the seasons, how they all continue on to create harmony and balance.

Life is a sacred circle. When we gather in a circle, the praying has already begun. When we gather in a circle, we communicate with each other and with Great Mystery, even without a word being spoken.

When do you gather in a circle with other people, and what do you notice about how it feels? What circles—with other people or creatures or living things—might you realize today?

25

BARTERING

Today, we should use these ancient teachings to live our lives in harmony with the plan that the Creator gave us. We are to do these things if we are to be natural people of the universe. . . . There are yet more teachings that can teach us how to live in ni-noo-do-da-di-win (harmony) with the creation.

—Eddie Benton Banai, Anishnabe

At one time in the not-so-distant past, bartering produced almost everything needed in a Native North American economy. Whatever one lacked could be traded for in an active intertribal system of barter. Centers of mass trade like Poverty Point, Cahokia, Chaco Canyon, and Celilo Falls were known far and wide by hundreds of tribes as places of abundant commerce.

Neighboring tribes consistently traded staples and other food items to make up for any lack they had and to add diversity to their diets. For example, desert floor tribes in the western United States who had an abundance of piñon nuts traded with neighboring tribes living in different climates, where oak trees and acorns were in vast supply. River nations on both continental coasts traded salmon for other items of value. Wampum shells in the northeastern coasts and pipestone in the central plains were traded among tribal peoples. Horses were traded, as well as dried food and precious stones such as turquoise, in the Southwest.

Indigenous America found value both in intertribal relationships and relatedness to the community of creation: to the land and all it produced naturally. Vegetables, salt, medicines, and hundreds of other items were freely traded between Indigenous Americans. But generally, a tribe's own lands produced the wealth needed for them to survive.

Bartering takes place very infrequently anymore in America, at least on a large-scale basis. But in small communities, it does go on. One person raises bees for honey, and another keeps chickens for eggs; another makes wooden bowls, while still another does automobile repair. It is difficult to make a living by bartering unless everyone does it. But in a supplemental way, bartering can enrich our lives and give us a sense of pride that paying cash for everything might not. Bartering systems remind us how much we actually rely on the Earth for our needs. Rather than thinking of a store as the supplier of all our needs, we begin to turn toward each other.

Over time, the land taught Indigenous people how to keep everything in balance: how much to use and how much to leave. This is a lesson we need to learn quickly.

What are the ways you are leaving nature her fair share? With whom could you barter, and with what services or items?

26
INTENTIONAL RELATIONSHIP

Look! Look! Look deep into nature and you will understand everything.

—Albert Einstein

The fact that all creation is connected implies the possibility not just of familiarity but of deliberate relationship. We should make room for the notion that all creation, in some way, expresses the image of Creator. In other words, there is something of God in all of God's creation. There is something of the universal life force in all of life. When we understand the level of sacredness this implies, we live out these relationships intentionally.

When I awake in the morning and drink my first glass of water for the day, I look at the water. Hopefully it is good, pure water, but regardless, I realize this water is a gift. This water is prolonging my life. This water connects me to the Earth. Our relationship is sacred, and I give thanks to the water and to Creator.

With my first bite of food, I think about what I am eating. I understand the sacrifice made by the plant or the animal to give me life. My life is connected to their death. There is a sacred relationship between myself and the food I eat.

I also think about how the food got to my plate. Who grew it? Who picked it? Who processed it? What land was used to grow it? What was the cost to the plants and animals who used to inhabit that land? How were their lives disrupted?

Without ever knowing them, I understand that there is a direct relationship with every aspect of how my food came to be. I have a sacred relationship with my food, the water used to grow it, the people who harvested it, and the wildlife who were displaced.

The breath of life, given by Great Mystery, is what ties all creation together. To take this into my heart and mind daily is to acknowledge my relationship to my world. If I fail to recognize the connection, I am simply not facing my own reality.

At your next meal, stop for a moment. Give intentional thought to your relationship to everything on your table.

27

IN A GOOD WAY

We learned about honesty and integrity—that the truth
matters . . . that you don't take shortcuts or play by your own
set of rules . . . and success doesn't count unless you earn it fair
and square.

—Michelle Obama

My experience among our most traditional people from dozens of
tribes tells me there is a dividing line in Indian country. Everyone is on one side of that line or the other. Although the line is
difficult to describe in just a few words, the most often used question about those who cross the line from the outside to the inside
is whether they come "in a good way."

A person either enters the world of traditional Native American
thoughts and practices by coming "in a good way"—or not.

The "good way" has to do with respect and honor and protocols.
You see, in Indian country, there are rules. No one has written
them down; they don't need to, but they are ironclad nevertheless.
And when these rules are violated, everyone will know about it.

And when you do things in a good way, people will know and understand that too.

Indigenous values are deeply held. Respecting elders, safeguarding the dignity of everyone having a voice, extending your relations beyond immediate family, showing humility, courage, generosity, hospitality, and honor—these are just some of these values. Such values are reinforced through story, and song, and ceremony, and especially just in the way a person "is." And the way a person "is" shows through the protocols they practice.

Do they pray—or do they simply go about the day as if they control everything? Do they honor elders by meeting their needs, listening to them, and bringing them gifts when asking for their advice—or do they disregard them and treat them poorly? Are the ceremonies they adopt given to them through wise mentors—or do they just appropriate what has been a practice among a particular tribe, clan, or family for generations? Do they share what they have with others—or do they hoard wealth and resources? Do their words and actions match—or do they say one thing but do another? These are questions, unspoken but real.

It has always been important in Indian country to know who comes in a good way and who does not. Families, villages, tribes, and whole worlds have been destroyed when people do not come in a good way. Tread lightly in Indian country.

Consider whether or not you are walking in a good way. Let that phrase, and its meaning, saturate your day.

28

PAW PRINTS

There are not enough Indians in the world to defeat the Seventh Cavalry.

—George Armstrong Custer

They say there are more bears on Kodiak Island in Alaska than people. When visitors arrive in Kodiak—usually after sitting through several canceled flights because of fog and inclement weather—they are greeted at the airport by a huge stuffed Kodiak bear: mouth open, teeth showing, and paws extended, with claws as long as my fingers reaching toward you in attack mode. The Kodiak brown bear is the largest carnivorous land mammal in the United States, sometimes measuring all of twelve feet from a back paw on the ground to an extended front paw. Welcome to Kodiak!

Children in schools on the island are taught how to respond if a bear approaches them. I worked for two years on Kodiak Island, and our four-year-old daughter learned that if she encountered a bear, she should make low tonal sounds, raise her coat above her head to make herself look larger than she was, and slowly back away.

Humor is one way of sharing a fearful reality. The story goes that old bear hunters tell newbies, "If you have six bullets in your gun, and you haven't stopped him after five, use the last one on yourself." Or "Be sure to hunt with someone slower than you; you can't outrun a Kodiak bear, but all you really need to do is outrun the guy you're with."

Everyone on the island has a bear story. I have mine. I thought I needed the Kodiak bear-hunting experience, so I secured my permit and scoped out what seemed to be good bear-hunting ground. Since I was hunting alone (not recommended), I decided to hunt from a tree. I thought if I found a tree that I could climb safely, and if I could climb up high enough, the bear could not pick me like an apple.

I sat in that tree at various times, waiting to see a bear. On the last day of hunting season, I took a tape measure with me to measure the bear if I got one—and to see how high up I was sitting in that tree. On the final morning, I came across something disturbing. There, in the snow in front of me, were large Kodiak bear paw tracks. They were enormous! I wear a size eleven snow boot, but I could still step inside one of the tracks so that both lengthwise and widthwise there was still a gap between my boot and the edge of the track.

A chill came over me. I walked over to my tree, which was just yards away from the bear tracks, and I measured the height of the branch where I had been sitting. It was nine feet seven inches from the ground. Without another thought, I turned around and went home.

Is there an obstacle in your life too large for you to handle? Accepting defeat and asking for help is sometimes wiser than what we mistake for courage.

29
HUMOR

A cheerful heart is good medicine.

—Proverbs 17:22

Indigenous people deal with some of their deepest problems through humor, especially self-deprecating humor. Having suffered genocide, forced assimilation, poverty, and disease, many Native people find humor a necessary coping tool. Humor also has a central role to play in Native American spirituality. The sincerest form of spirituality among American Indian life is to be a "real human being"—meaning one who seeks to be humble and know their place as a created being on this Earth.

Indigenous trickster stories teach people *not* to try to be anything more than a simple, humble human being. Tricksters are mythical creatures found in the stories of most Indigenous tribes. Aboriginal stories often use tricksters to explain how things came to be and to teach lessons of morality. The stories are sometimes regionally interchangeable, with different names given to the trickster. Many lessons can be learned from trickster stories, but the most glaring themes are probably to be happy with yourself, just as you are, and be grateful for all you have been given lest the trickster fool you into becoming a target for someone else's schemes.

Old rivalries often result in tribes or bands focusing their humor on the other group having more problems than themselves. For example, I first heard this joke from a Lakota of the Rosebud Sioux Reservation, who was teasing a person from another Sioux band, the neighboring Pine Ridge Reservation, about their poverty. The joke goes like this: Did you hear about the two Indians walking down the highway between Pine Ridge and Rosebud? Each is coming from his own reservation when they see each other from far off on the horizon. The guy from Rosebud notices the guy from Pine Ridge is walking with a limp. The Rosebud guy watches him get closer and closer, and finally, when they see each other from a fairly close distance, the guy from Rosebud sees the other guy is wearing one old, badly worn, duct-taped sneaker on only one of his feet. "Hey, looks like you lost a shoe," the guy from Rosebud yells. "No," the Pine Ridge fellow yells back, "I found one!"

Another classic joke throughout Indian country is about "Indian cars": old vehicles, falling apart, and said to be held together by duct tape and baling wire. It's said, "If all four tires match, it's not a real Indian car." There is even a popular song called "Indian Car" by Native artist Keith Secola. Sung at various functions throughout Indian country, the song has become something of a national anthem for Indian humor.

Poor housing, food scarcity, low incomes, and unemployment all plague Indian country. But humor is one way to focus on what is really important—namely, life itself.

Today, as you consider life's problems, look for the humor in your situation.

30

MY PORCH SWING

Nature shrinks as capital grows. The growth of the market cannot solve the very crisis it creates.

—Vandana Shiva

I often retreat to my porch swing for solace. On our current farm, the porch swing is in a good place: it hangs on the back porch, facing the Coastal Mountain Range to our west.

But not long ago, on the little farm where we used to live about twenty miles from here, it was a front porch swing, and sitting on it reminded me of agricultural practices that weaken the Earth. Our front porch was surrounded by our neighbor's large filbert orchards on three sides. Those filberts, also known as hazelnuts, are typical of the industrial agriculture that took over some of the most fertile soil on the continent: Oregon's Willamette Valley. Row after row in an endless gaze, the filbert trees stand—and eventually fall due to filbert blight, a disease caused by unsustainable practices and soil leached with herbicides.

Wild filberts are native to our area; I guess that's why their domesticated cousins grow so well in this climate. But really, a filbert does not want to be a tree. It sends from its roots many small trees, similar to the way that bushes and hedges might wander. I think human attempts to tame these trees may be a part of the problem: by trimming them down to one trunk, we try to make them into something they are not.

At Eloheh Center for Earth Justice and Eloheh Farm & Seeds, we engage principles of permaculture, biomimicry, and traditional Indigenous knowledge to grow our fruits, vegetables, and open-pollinated seed stock. We are one of several organic havens in the midst of monocultural, industrialized, agricultural blight.

The stark difference I used to face daily—between our organic practices and those that maintain the filbert orchards—provoked many deep thoughts from my porch swing. I clearly saw a dying, unsustainable, and bleak world. I wonder, How can people ignore the sacredness of this place?

Even today while sitting on my new porch swing, I wonder, What would it take for my neighbors to see the sacred Earth as God's own creation? Sacred to the Kalapuyan people since time immemorial. Sacred to me now. How could I help others see the contrast between these two different ways of living in the world?

I want to put out a grand invitation to my neighbors and beyond: instead of destroying the land of our grandchildren, please come sit with me for a while, on my porch swing.

What do you think about the world when looking out your window or sitting on your porch? What are your hopes? Do something today to lessen the gap between what is and what could be.

PART FOUR

SEEING AND NAMING INDIGENOUS SPLENDOR

31

LIVED EXPERIENCE

If you carry a cat by the tail, you'll learn something that you can learn in no other way.

—Mark Twain

Indigenous peoples value lived experience over dry knowledge. In Indian country, true knowledge is not so much about facts as it is about gaining an understanding or even a revelation from creation, a dream, or an experience. From a young age until now, I've learned that knowing must translate from the head to the heart and the hands and the feet in order to be respected as true knowledge or perhaps even considered wisdom. What we do about what we know determines who we are.

I am honored to be a keeper of several traditional items and ceremonies. To become a keeper of a particular tradition, song, or ceremony means one must have been mentored in it, understand it, practice it, steward it, and know when it is appropriate to enact. I was taught these particular ceremonies and traditions by elders who were considered keepers of the various sacred things. They taught me to observe closely when they were doing a task.

Even more importantly, the elders taught me to *not* ask too many questions. Later, if I was patient in each process, I would have the opportunity to demonstrate what I had learned. And I would be corrected when needed. The elders often told me to pray about what I was learning and to think about these things. I was also told that my questions—which I kept to myself—could be answered through prayer.

This learning style was very different from my training in college and graduate school. In those institutions, I was certified as an expert based on my knowledge of certain facts that could be verified and transferred to other contexts. How I kept the knowledge, or whether I even used it in life, were of little concern. Prayer was a part of my particular Western training, but prayer is often understood a bit differently in that context—as if it is done to gain something.

Prayers in the Indigenous ways are mostly about giving thanks and offering hope that I can become a better person. Prayers are offered in that spirit of humility, asking so that my questions will eventually be answered if I wait and keep alert to each moment in my life.

When learning a new skill or new knowledge, make it your goal to watch and listen. What might it look like to hold your questions until you have had time to meditate or pray on them?

32

MARRIED TO THE LAND

Thou shalt no more be termed Forsaken; neither shall thy land any more be termed Desolate: but thou shalt be called Hephzibah, and thy land Beulah: for the Lord delighteth in thee, and thy land shall be married.

—Isaiah 62:4 (KJV)

Edith and I have been married now for over thirty years, and we know each other quite well. But sometimes she still surprises me. Marriage involves both deep knowledge of another and the willingness to be surprised by them.

The prophet Isaiah's words reveal a clear image of people at home with their land. His words even suggest the idea of being married to—or "Beulah" with—the land.

How do people become married to the land? What intimacies of love and commitment and daily relationship emerge? The degree to which we are willing to spend time alone with the land may determine the level of intimacy. What we are willing to risk in order to have a deep relationship with the land makes a difference. Is our time superficial? Is it overbearing, seeing ourselves as the center of everything? Or do we gently and tenderly continue to seek out the relationship on the land's own terms, understanding the wholeness of the community of creation and our small and temporary part in it? An intimate relationship with the land is one of humility.

When a people are married to the land, both land and people become part of a healing process. Intimacy is required to know one's land. There is a courtship prior to a marriage, usually with much time passing. We would not treat something so sacred with superficiality and casualness.

In the case of America's Indigenous people, this relationship has lasted from time immemorial. Indigenous people of a particular land became married to it in a very real way. They would be forever shaped by that land, even if they were later separated from that land.

Although I now live far from my ancestor's Cherokee homeland, when I visit the Smoky Mountains, something deep and primordial within me responds. My wife, who is Eastern Shoshone, says she experiences something similar in her visits to the mountain ranges in the American West.

Imagine the relationship that is possible with the land on which you live. Imagine learning what a particular people married to the land for untold generations might yield.

As you visit the land around you, try imagining it as the beginning of a courtship. How might you also acknowledge and get to know the people who have been married to it for so long before you?

33

CARETAKERS

It is essential to show special care for indigenous communities and their cultural traditions. They are not merely one minority among others, but should be the principal dialogue partners, especially when large projects affecting their land are proposed. For them, land is not a commodity but rather a gift from God and from their ancestors who rest there, a sacred space with which they need to interact if they are to maintain their identity and values. When they remain on their land, they themselves care for it best.

—Pope Francis

Pope Francis created a wonderful document in *Laudato Si'*: the second encyclical that called all people of the world to care for our common home, the Earth. Unfortunately, most people of the world will not read it. Those who do read *Laudato Si'* may develop important moral teachings as a result. Yet this process will take time we may not have.

The urgency of Earth's crisis requires we go beyond moral teaching.

If the help of Indigenous peoples is to be sought, actions are needed now. Confession of the wrongs done to Indigenous peoples around the world must include acts of restitution, restoration, and empowerment. Papal authority affords a "bully pulpit" that could be used to confess specific wrongs done around the world and ask for the help of the world's Indigenous peoples.

While I appreciate the pope's concern, he stops short of what is actually needed. Not only should Indigenous peoples be shown "special care"; they must be restored as the West's primary moral teachers. Most of the capital that the West now possesses—including the wealth owned by churches—comes as a result of the oppression and attempted destruction of Indigenous peoples. The debt owed to Indigenous peoples not only includes "special care" but empowerment: elevation to positions of authority. Indigenous leaders can help us secure humanity's privilege as the primary caretakers of Earth.

Pope Francis and other world leaders could lead the way. They could dedicate a decade demanding our direct involvement in restoring the community of creation. They could institute environmental action as a new spiritual discipline.

Organizations wishing to seriously take on the challenge of climate change need to expose the fallacies of the Western worldview and the theologies that result. They need to empower Indigenous people, who will guide us to a better future. The work must be done faithfully and fervently for the healing of the community of creation.

Let us hope and pray that the community of creation will be forgiving.

What organizations do you belong to that could install and empower Indigenous people as moral teachers and leaders? How could you seek out Indigenous leaders as authorities?

34

ETHNIC IDENTITY

I should not have to prove my ethnicity to anyone. I know who I am.

—Christina Aguilera

We have created a thing called "race." Regardless of whether or not you come from one or more of the major racialized social categories, we all have ancestral ethnicities—be they Celtic, Norse, Zulu, or Aztec. Ethnicities sometimes relate to a nation, sometimes to a people or tribal group. Ethnicity is fluid but real.

My spouse and I grew up very differently, although we both are descended from Native Americans and European ethnicities. My childhood and most of my young adult life were spent searching for my Native American identity in books, family stories, and the wisdom of my Indian friends' parents. My own Indigenous identity could have easily become lost amid the expectations of colonial assimilation.

Edith, on the other hand, was raised on the Wind River Indian Reservation in Wyoming. Even as a child, she was exposed to an abundance of Indigenous tradition, culture, and wisdom. Although her presumed identity was all around her and in her, as a young adult, she often resisted owning her own Native identity.

The dynamics of our different struggles are not uncommon among Native Americans—or, I suppose, any people group. Some people, like me, are given a thimbleful of Indigenous blood and culture. From there, they must choose to participate somewhere, in degrees between indifference or a lifelong pursuit of indigeneity. Others like my wife, who grew up immersed in Indianness, sometimes resist—only to appreciate their Indigenous identity later in life. Or sometimes never.

Whatever way one comes at their own Indigenous identity, each person has much to add to the cultural splendor that has been given as a birthright to the people of that particular land.

Take a DNA test, or read a book, or talk to a relative. Do something today to reconnect to your own ethnic identity.

35

BERRIES

It's not what you take but what you leave behind that defines greatness.

—Edward Gardner

I love listening to my wife reflect on her years growing up on the reservation. Edith comes alive when she talks of swimming in the river, heading up the mountains as a family to cut the annual Christmas tree, and riding horses all over the reservation. I wish I could say, like she can, that I'd had the pleasure of riding my horse to the general store and parking it at the hitching post in front of the store! Although she has sad stories too, many of Edith's memories brim with wisdom and joy, and she now passes on these stories to our children and grandchildren.

Of all the stories from her childhood, none make her happier to tell than those surrounding berries. To Plains tribal people, berries are a rare treat. Whether they are bull berries or buffalo berries or chokecherries or any other variety, these jewels make life fun and interesting. They are fun to pick, especially for the little children, and interesting because they can be eaten in a number of different ways and used in various recipes. And don't forget that berries are highly nutritious as well.

Invariably, when our family goes out to pick berries, Edith reminds the kids—and now the grandkids—"Remember, these berries are not just for us. The birds and mice and other creatures get to have some too."

Then she talks about what her older brother, Tom, would tell them as kids. Tom was traditional. As a small child, Edith would listen carefully to her older brother's teachings. Back then, she says, "I didn't think of them as 'teachings.' I just thought of them as things that Tom would say."

These days, she quotes her brother's teachings to our berry-picking helpers. As we pick, she reminds us, like her brother used to remind her, "Don't pick all the berries from the top: those are for the birds. And don't pick all the ones at the bottom: those are for the small animals that can't reach high up. Pick mostly from the middle: those are the berries for us."

And we do.

How might you "pick from the middle" today so that the rest of creation has enough? And how might you pass along that wisdom to future generations?

36
MAKING RELATIVES

My father literally fought his entire life to ensure the inclusion of all people because he understood that we were intertwined and connected together in humanity.

—Bernice King

When I first moved to Anadarko, Oklahoma, sometimes called the "Indian capital of the nation," I knew no one. A Kiowa elder mother who lived there, and who had lost her adult son to cancer the prior year, felt God tell her that she would be given another son. After a year of grieving was completed, I showed up, and she asked to adopt me as her son.

In days past, when someone lost a child or parent or other relative, this type of Indian adoption, called "making a relative," was a way to bring both happiness and that role function back into play. It was a covenantal agreement. In a way, it was a method of restoring balance and, if one was fortunate, restoring happiness.

I hope I became a good son to her. I sought her and her husband's advice on big decisions, attended ceremonies and important events with them, and offered my help whenever needed. In all these things, I was learning the ways of the Kiowa. My Kiowa father once told a large group of people, "Randy is Cherokee, but we made a Kiowa out of him." Though I wouldn't claim to have reached that honored status, I can say I have loved the Kiowa as a people, and I appreciate all I have been given by them.

I have gained a lot of relatives over the years through Indian adoption from several tribes. And I have adopted a few relatives myself. In the Indian way, adoption is more than just a symbolic gesture; it is a necessary means to include others. Everyone in the tribe has a role and a relative status. These customs are maintained so there is no role confusion. Everyone understands what is expected of them, and everyone works together from within those roles.

The making-of-a-relative ceremony is a happy and generous time for everyone. A feast is made, gifts are given away, and jokes and laughter permeate the event, as does solemnity. In these events, everyone knows that the community has become much fuller through inclusion.

What can you do to include someone in your life today who seems to be on the outside?

37
POW WOW

When the Pow Wow is over tonight darling, come on over to my tipi. We will watch the sun come up together.

—Native American Round Dance Song

A Pow Wow is a social event where Native American cultural splendor is displayed at its finest. Pow Wows can be found in all fifty states and nearly all Canadian provinces, and they are public events to which everyone in the community is invited. To the casual observer, it might be difficult to discern differences between a Traditional Dancer and a Fancy Dancer or a Chicken Dance song from a Grass Dance song. To the uninitiated, a Pow Wow can feel like grand, chaotic hoopla. But the invisibility of a pattern to outside eyes doesn't mean it's not there. Within that circle, everyone is observing a fairly strict and established order. By observing traditions passed on now for many years, the dancers move in patterns, and rhythm, and a deep form that may be invisible to newcomers.

Pow Wows were not originally intertribal. I have heard elders from various Western Plains tribes explain the origins of the Pow

Wow, each with its own nuance depending on their tribe, but with enough similarity to see the common thread. According to one Shoshone version, in the old days, each clan would perform its own dances and songs for the other clans in that tribe.

At that time, the women would stand around the outer edge of the circle while the men danced, "bobbing" their knees to the drumbeat. In time, tribes began performing the dances together. With more and more intertribal friendships and connections, the various dances and songs that accompanied them were shared among the various tribes. The many dance styles and songs shared with each other included women's and children's songs and dances as well. Eventually, some general categories of dances became the most popular, which now constitute those of the modern intertribal Pow Wow.

What might seem chaotic to the uninitiated can often reflect a deep kind of order. Based on generations of tradition, those within the circle are moving and dancing together. Nature also has an order or circle that is often missed by the casual observer. I suppose, in some ways, the dances and songs reflect that too.

Humility and the desire to learn bring one inside any circle. Today, try to cultivate humility and a willingness to learn from within any circle you inhabit.

38

SWEET POTATOES, CHICKENS, STARS, AND A BLUE MOON

For the most part, contemporary historians have proceeded from the presumption that modern people are different from and superior to those who came before—especially those designated as "primitives." Distortions and incomplete and even dishonest renderings of the past are found in many modern accounts of ancient peoples and contemporary "primitive" peoples; these accounts serve to reinforce the sense of difference and to distance moderns from unflattering legacies of the past.

—John Mohawk, Seneca

A blue moon is out tonight. The old adage informs us that a blue moon doesn't happen very often. I could always google how often and why it is called a blue moon, but right now, at three thirty in the morning, that does not interest me.

As I look up at the bright orange moon, I am both captured by its beauty and amazed at the amount of light it gives off. I look around the sky and I see a few familiar sights: Orion, Cassiopeia, the Big Dipper (or is that the Little Dipper?). These constellations have been the subject of myth and legend in nearly every culture.

The Polynesians, especially those of Hawaii, have always been great navigators. They relied on these same stars and others to take them across one-third of the Earth's surface, or what we now call the Pacific Ocean. A seven-thousand-mile journey and back on the Pacific Ocean is a feat in any vessel, but especially one without a motor! Controversy surrounds these facts, but a good argument can be made that Hawaiian navigators reached South America years before Europeans. Radiocarbon-dated chicken bones, native to the Pacific Islands and not to South America, have shown this plausible fact. Apparently, large Hawaiian double-hulled *waka* carried not only a bunch of Hawaiians but also chickens, as well as other food supplies.

But what would have sustained them on their return voyage?

Sweet potatoes, a very rich source of vitamins and minerals, originated in Central and South America and not Hawaii, according to DNA samplings. But archaeologists have discovered sweet potatoes in Polynesia dating around 1000 CE. In addition to all the scientific work behind radiocarbon dating and potato DNA, there is a linguistic clue as well. One of the Polynesian words for "sweet potato" is *kuumala*. The word for "sweet potato" in ancient Quechua, a native language of the Peruvian Andes, is *kumara*.

I think we underestimate the intelligence of Indigenous people when we use the word *primitive* to describe them. *Potato, potado, kuumala, kumara*—let's call the whole thing remarkable! And to think, all these ancient people stared at the same moon as me. I wonder what they were thinking.

When you read about "primitive" societies, remember to search out their great contributions. How can you give credit where credit is due?

39

BEAR DREAMS

The only thing we have to fear is fear itself.
—Franklin Delano Roosevelt

Among some of our tribes, you must not talk about bears or wear anything from a bear unless you have had dreams about bears. Some tribes forbid the eating of bears because they believe the bear people to be our closest relatives. Tribal stories reinforce these practices and others concerning bear power.

To some, bears represent our greatest fears. I am one of those fortunate enough to have had bear dreams, so I can talk about it.

At one point in my life, I suffered terrible angst over a particular fear. This fear was so deep that I had never shared it with anyone. After more than a year of distress over this issue, I had, over a period of several weeks, a series of bear dreams.

The first three dreams were practically the same. I was going hunting for a bear. When I would finally come upon the bear, the bear would explain to me that I didn't really want to shoot that bear and that I was really looking for *another* bear—one much greater than the one standing before me. Then *that* bear would tell me where to find the great bear, who by reputation was so strong and so fierce. At about that point, I would wake up.

As I said, I had the same dream three times. In my fourth and final bear dream, I finally met up with the great, fearsome bear—except he wasn't so fearsome. In fact, he wasn't at all what I had expected!

The mighty and powerful bear was old and decrepit. He stood before me, looking at me as if to say, "There is nothing left to fear." In my dream, I put down my rifle, and he simply wandered off. Then I woke up.

Since then, whenever that particular fear arises in me—which has been seldom after the dreams, and now practically never—I remember my bear dreams. And the fear subsides.

Pay attention to your dreams. Sometimes they are just unprocessed thoughts, and sometimes they are very sacred directions. Trust that you will know the difference.

40

TURNING TORNADOS

He got up, rebuked the wind and said to the waves, "Quiet! Be
still!" Then the wind died down and it was completely calm.
—Mark 4:39 (NIV)

Jake, my Kiowa dad, told me a story once about when he was just
a young guy. Jake was in his eighties when he told me the story.

He and his family were living in the shadow of Rainy Mountain, in the place now known as Oklahoma. There had been a
series of tornados that season, and his father had dug a shelter for
the family to secure themselves during such scares.

One morning, a tornado was coming their way. The tornado
was making what seemed a beeline toward their home. Jake's father
secured the kids in the underground tornado shelter and then went
out to meet the tornado.

Jake said he was concerned about his dad leaving the shelter and
the danger that awaited him outside. So Jake ran out of the shelter
just in time to see the tornado slowly making its way toward them.

"I'll never forget what happened next," Jake told me, the
memory brightening his eyes. He heard his dad speaking loudly,

with a voice of authority. He heard his father say directly to the tornado, "You need to go through another way. There are Kiowa people here, and we don't want you here. Now go!"

To Jake's amazement, the tornado immediately changed its course and bypassed them. He saw it happen, and he told me he would never forget it.

I only heard the story, and I will never forget it. That story was told to me over thirty years ago. It is as fresh to me now as the day Jake shared it.

What questions come to mind when you hear this story and think about our relationship with nature? Write them down and think on them.

PART FIVE

REALIZING THE AMERICAN DREAM IS AN INDIGENOUS NIGHTMARE

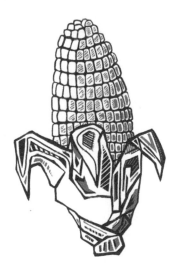

41

LIVING WITH NATURE

We cannot know the whole truth, which belongs to God alone, but our task nevertheless is to seek to know what is true. And if we offend gravely enough against what we know to be true, as by failing badly enough to deal affectionately and responsibly with our land and our neighbors, truth will retaliate with ugliness, poverty, and disease.

—Wendell Berry

As settlers began to move in, Native people's crucial food supplies became more and more scarce. These food sources had been available to them for millennia and had kept them in a symbiotic balance with the land. Indigenous hunters had to travel farther distances, which sometimes resulted in competition among themselves and other tribes. This competition often led to conflicts and sometimes even resulted in wars.

The very land itself meant something quite different to the newcomer than it did to the host people. Something was missing. The difficulty, as the Natives saw it, was with the settlers themselves and their failure to tread lightly, with humility and respect, on the land. The settlers wanted to live *on* the land, but the host people lived *with* the land. Living on the land means objectifying the land and natural resources and being shortsighted concerning the future. Living with the land means respecting the natural balance.

To Indigenous peoples, the problems of a Western worldview are obvious. The way of life demonstrated by Western peoples leads to alienation from the Earth, from others, and from all of creation. This lifestyle creates a false bubble called "Western civilization," which people of the West think will protect them from future calamity. This false hope is detached from all experience and reality.

The problem is that the Western system *itself* is what brings the calamity. There is little doubt that much of what we are experiencing today as so-called natural disasters have their origin in human carelessness.

How do we avoid the impending disaster brought on by a settler lifestyle of living *on* the land and against nature? The answer is simple: we learn to live *with* nature.

What areas in your daily life cause calamity in nature? Choose at least one and make a change so that you begin to live *with* the land, not just *on* it.

42

MYTHS THAT TELL OUR STORY

Our nation was born in genocide. . . . We are perhaps the only nation which tried as a matter of national policy to wipe out its indigenous population. Moreover, we elevated that tragic experience into a noble crusade. Indeed, even today we have not permitted ourselves to reject or feel remorse for this shameful episode.

—Martin Luther King Jr.

America tells a story about itself. It's a story based on freedom, equality, opportunity, and fairness. These imagined values spin a narrative that America is *the* place where the divine story uniquely comes together with the human story and unfolds as divine providence. We could call it the myth of American exceptionalism. Together, these notions serve as a location for the American dream. This false narrative has become, to many people, a real place. But the place they imagine is formless.

Western minds think of "the land of the free" in terms of *all* land: a vague place, a nostalgic and fuzzy landscape. America, according to the American dream, is the place where all these wonderful traits are sewn into the national story—and not in any one place, but rather "from sea to shining sea." When Americans think of land in the abstract realm, it becomes universalized, meaning "all land." But all land, which is concretely inconceivable, means no land. So land becomes not a real place but an abstract reality.

American exceptionalism—and its progeny, the American dream—contains an ethic of extreme competition, to the point where Americans believe we must fight (read "kill others") to be free and retain our divinely bestowed values. Native Americans were killed by the millions to create this myth.

And yet the greatest leaders of all time—Jesus, Buddha, Guru Nanak, Black Kettle, Mahatma Gandhi, Dorothy Day, Martin Luther King Jr., and others—call us to peace through very different narratives. Each had the ability to observe the worst of life but tell a story that makes us better. Each told a better story.

How do we hear a better story to replace the half-truths of history? We listen to people with a different view who tell another side of history.

The fact remains that we live our lives according to our myths—our narratives. We find what fits in such a myth, and we make that part of our own personal story. We leave out the histories that *don't* fit our myths, like genocide and ecocide. But when we leave out any part of the story, we distort reality.

America has taught people to live against each other and against nature and has justified and even glorified these actions. We have a long way to go to counteract the American myth and reverse the tide. We have a long way to go to accept our reality.

How could you counter one of the myths your country lives by? Will you commit to reading several books in the coming year by Indigenous authors?

43

DOCTRINE OF DISCOVERY

And we make, appoint, and depute you and your said heirs and successors lords of them with full and free power, authority, and jurisdiction of every kind.

—Pope Alexander VI, "Inter Caetera," 1493

For more than five centuries, Indigenous peoples across the world had their land, labor, and resources stolen and were systematically denied their human rights. What made this massive theft conceivable to the settlers who enacted the violence? The answer: the doctrine of discovery and the international laws based on it.

The doctrine of discovery originated with the Christian church and was based on Christian Scripture, including passages like the Great Commission, the divine mandate to rule in Romans 13, and the Exodus narrative of a covenantal people justified in taking possession of land. The doctrine of discovery is still enshrined in US law today. A US Supreme Court decision in the case of *Johnson v. McIntosh* and several other cases perpetuate the doctrine.

Once the idea of supremacy was solidified in Catholicism, it became socially acceptable for all of Christianity. In this case,

White, Western European supremacy, under the guise of a mandate from God, could be justified, and America's host people, along with the whole Earth, stood in peril. In the Americas, that idea became full-throated White supremacy: the belief that White people were superior to all other peoples of the Earth. Racism, then, became the tool of White supremacy to inflict upon North American Natives an inferior social status.

The results of White supremacy upon the Indigenous peoples in North America, especially as it played out in a capitalistic society, were poverty, disease, and death. The primary form of asset in North America was land. White settlers took that stolen land (capital) from Native Americans and used it to create their own wealth. In the process, Native Americans found themselves trying to adapt to a land-based, capitalistic society with few or no assets.

Today, Native Americans remain among the most affected by poverty, disease, and early death, all of which continue the colonial legacy. Yet despite more than five hundred years of horrendous theft and genocide, we are still here.

When you think of this tragic history, how could your sadness and remorse turn into allyship for Native people's survival? How might you cultivate a sincere desire to learn from such a people? We are still here.

44

WAR AND PEACE

Pocahontas portrayals tell the saga of Indian-white relations. At first the Indians are hostile and dangerous. But key figures like Pocahontas bring reconciliation. Eventually the Indians are subdued and (according to the myth) integrated into the new nation . . . (symbolized by Pocahontas' marriage and baptism). . . . Pocahontas speaks of the stealing of native lands and the genocide of native peoples, America's original sin.

—Howard Snyder

Stealing land, resources, and ultimately power are the initial goals of colonization. Remember the force it takes to obtain these goals. The militarization of the Western mind has become part of that national mythos. Justice, when it comes to imperial military logic, seems to have very little bearing.

The occupying military force here, in the land that became the United States of America, has barely seen a handful of years without military conflict. This has created a culture of violence and had a tremendous effect on the American psyche. Competition, the misuse of power, violence, and division have become the new normal. Americans are always in conflict partly because Americans are satisfied with a myth that has created a false sense of peace and harmony.

Ancient Native Americans attempted to avoid wars as best they could. They developed numerous practical strategies for peacemaking. Many movies and novels portray America's Indigenous people as bloodthirsty savages, but these bear little resemblance to the people who actually lived and to what we know of historical facts.

Yes, there were Native American wars. Yes, sometimes extreme violence was used against others. But in general, Native Americans waged war differently than the settlers did. To my knowledge, no wars concerning religion were fought. And the idea of war, in a Native American mind, was most often to balance out an injustice, to demonstrate acts of courage, or to ensure one's people's survival during hard times—not to kill as many people as possible and take over another nation's lands.

Our national myth has relished our wars, and Hollywood has made a ton of money feeding us the myths we want to hear about them.

What wars have been fought in your lifetime? Examine their causes and compare them with the ones listed concerning America's Indigenous peoples. What might be strategies for peace in our time?

45

ANCIENT CONTRIBUTIONS

> Having grown separately for millennia, the Americas were a bound-
> less sea of novel ideas, dreams, stories, philosophies, religions,
> moralities, discoveries and all the other products of the mind.
> —Kevin Baker, in a review of *1491: Vanished Americans*

Progress. Civilization. Modernity. The European invasion and west-
ward migration are often described by words such as these. The
Western goal of progress for aboriginals throughout the centuries was to "civilize" them. Yet the irony is that advanced civilizations already existed among the first Americans when the settlers
arrived. Indigenous peoples had developed systems of science,
language, rhetoric, mathematics, medicine, environmental ecolo-
gies, architecture, and economic systems. Most Europeans simply
didn't recognize Indigenous civilization as such.

Did you know some Native Americans were performing dentistry and brain surgery and that they developed a host of medicines still in use today? Do you realize that about 60 percent of the
world's foods today came from the Americas, and at precontact,
there were an estimated 5,000 varieties of corn and 3,500 varieties

of potatoes? All corn is "Indian corn"; and all potatoes originated in the Americas.

Have you heard of the large precontact cities in the Americas, such as Cahokia, El Mirador, and Chaco Canyon? Great civilizations thrived in America with unparalleled techniques. Here are a few:

- microagriculture and macroenvironmental management including ecology, xeriscape, agronomy, botany, forestry, raised beds, and naturally fertilized gardens
- sustainable architecture including passive solar heating and water capture systems
- humanities including psychology, philosophy, religion, rhetoric, languages, the arts, and ethics
- sciences including math, medicines, surgery, dentistry, the leeching of poisonous foods to make them edible, and healthy waste disposal
- urban planning, democratic governments, education systems, intercontinental economic trade, and complex peacemaking strategies

People frequently ask me why they have never been taught about the great Native American civilizations or their contributions to the world. My answer is always the same: *You weren't supposed to know.* Our national myths have been designed—on purpose, with intent—so people never learn these things.

What could you do today to discover more about Native American civilizations during precontact? Many excellent books and resources are available for anyone ready to learn. Try *1491: New Revelations of the Americas before Columbus* by Charles C. Mann as a start.

46

DESTRUCTION

I have never known an Indian to kill a game animal that he did not require for his needs. And I have known few white hunters to stop while there was game to kill.

—Major James McLaughlin

In the early days of the fur trappers in the Pacific Northwest, my wife's people group, the Shoshone, inhabited much of what we know as Oregon, Idaho, Nevada, California, Wyoming, and parts of Montana. One of the ways they made their living was by hunting big game such as deer, antelope, bison, and bighorn sheep. As the nineteenth century arose, fur companies began sending out fur trappers and establishing forts as centers for business. The new visitors traveled the Indian trails and followed the rivers and streams, where they were easily observed by the Indigenous people.

The Shoshone and other Indians could not believe what they saw. As long as there were animals left to kill, the Westerners would kill them all day long. Then they'd leave the majority of the meat to rot on the prairie. The malicious destruction of big game for no other reason but sport was unimaginable to the Shoshone and other tribal peoples, who themselves depended on nature's abundance for their survival. The Shoshone and other tribes understood the disruption of the natural world that this represented. They knew that if left unchecked, such practices would eventually lead to starvation.

The correlation between treating nature and people as the "other" is striking. The earliest explorers and pilgrims in the Americas and in most parts of the world demonstrated what we would later call White supremacy. One fur trapper, Jim Beckwourth, recorded his party taking 488 Bannock Indian scalps in one day. His victims were of all ages and genders, and his party left not one man, woman, or child alive. Beckwourth wrongly assumed he had wiped out the whole Bannock tribe. This pattern of the destruction of Indigenous peoples has been repeated all over the world.

When Indigenous people resisted their own destruction, subjugation, or the theft of their lands, they were considered the problem. Those who oppressed them created narratives that justified their own actions, and these narratives became myths that inform the worldview of the settler-colonizer. Beckwourth's attempted genocide of Indigenous peoples, along with that of others, naturally incited resistance and retaliation.

The destruction of various people groups is horrible. And the assault on the community of creation may eventually result in far more serious retaliation from the Earth herself.

Read *An Indigenous People's History of the United States* by Roxanne Dunbar Ortiz.

47

TOWARD RESPECT

American history is longer, larger, more various, more beautiful,
and more terrible than anything anyone has ever said about it.
—James Baldwin

How we view history informs our worldview for today and the
future. We turn our view of history into our present reality. When
teaching history courses to college and graduate students, I always
began with this claim: "There is no such thing as history—only
histories."

We should always ask this question: Who is telling the story
and why? Winners may write history, but our worldview should be
shaped as much by what the losers of history had to say. We must
try to hear those often-vanquished voices. And certainly, we should
create room to hear the voice of the Earth itself. When it comes to
war and exploitation, the Earth's voice is seldom considered.

Ultimately, a utilitarian view of creation results in wanton
destruction of the Earth for material gain. This attitude often crosses
the realm of nature to people. In fact, the way the Western world
has historically treated the Earth and the way it has treated Black,

Indigenous, and People of Color (BIPOC) populations—especially women—show remarkable parallels. A highly utilitarian view of people may explain why human life is valued so little in businesses that poison the Earth and humanity (most often the poor and communities of color). Consider the similarities: Nature, women, and people of color have all been objectified, exploited, and controlled. Nature, women, and people of color have been used for pleasure, expected to produce, and raped.

Our view of creation may determine why international trade is accompanied by a propensity toward violence, wars, and even genocide. The poorest and most marginalized suffer the most from corporate extraction of the Earth's natural resources. Such actions often result in wholesale racial and economic injustice. If those in the modern world do not understand or respect diversity in creation, it is not difficult to see why diversity would not be of any value when considering other humans.

There is a definite connection to how a society views the Earth, including the whole community of creation, and how it values human life.

The cure for objectification is respecting our relationship with the whole community of creation. In what tangible ways can you build on your relationship and show respect to nature today?

48

THE TRAUMA AND THE CURE

As for the vast mainland, which is ten times larger than all Spain. . . . We are sure that our Spaniards, with their cruel and abominable acts, have devastated the land and exterminated the rational people who fully inhabited it. We can estimate very surely and truthfully that in the forty years that have passed, with the infernal actions of the Christians, there have been unjustly slain more than twelve million men, women, and children. In truth, I believe without trying to deceive myself that the number of the slain is more like fifteen million.

—Father Bartolomé de Las Casas

How does a people group recover from trauma? How do they come back from displacement from their homes, complete change in their lifestyle and diet, forced subjugation, loss of loved ones, loss of traditions, and banishment of their religion?

Indigenous psychologist and writer Eduardo Duran, along with many others, believe most Native Americans are affected by postcolonial stress disorder (PCSD). PCSD describes the snowballing result of the effects of a people group living generation after generation with post-traumatic stress disorder. This very real sense of loss may have traveled down through the generations—and not just through story or shame or silence but through something as fundamental as our DNA. The results of the loss are verifiable: poverty, chronic disease, addiction, early death, high suicide rates. Generational PTSD leads to PCSD.

Yet if Indigenous people carry within us the trauma of genocide over generations, we also carry the cure—not just for ourselves, but for the whole Earth. The wisdom of survival of Indigenous people, who have suffered so much, offers the key to healing our world. The values kept since time immemorial are the same ones that will heal this Earth.

A harmonious worldview. Mutual respect. Generosity. Hospitality. Inclusion. Relatedness to all creation. Cooperation. Wisdom. Humor. These are the sureties that we need today to heal ourselves, the Earth, and the whole community of creation.

Explore these values in your mind and heart. Exercise at least one of them today.

49

TREAD LIGHTLY

Every part of this soil is sacred in the estimation of my people. Every hillside, every valley, every plain and grove, has been hallowed by some sad or happy event in days long vanished. . . . The very dust upon which you now stand responds more lovingly to their footsteps than yours, because it is rich with the blood of our ancestors, and our bare feet are conscious of the sympathetic touch.

—Chief Seattle, Duwamish and Suquamish

The ancient Indigenous people I descend from are referred to as mound builders, and locating ancient Cherokee mounds has become one of my hobbies. On one trip, driving from Tennessee to Alabama, I noticed an elementary school sitting on top of an ancient Cherokee village mound. This was the fourth school I have seen that was built on top of a mound; it's an irony I always find unsettling.

At one time, mound-building cultures built great cities throughout more than half the continent. The area around the mounds grew fields of corn, beans, squash, and sunflowers. The rivers and creeks would flood those fields in the late winter and spring and then recede, leaving a layer of silt to fertilize the fields for the next planting. Fall harvests were stored high up on the mound, in the council house.

The council house of every ancient Cherokee town sat upon a mound. In it was our sacred fire. Council houses were a combination church, social hall, and statehouse. Everyone in the town was welcome there, including the children, and everyone approached it with reverence and respect.

Our Cherokee culture was highly developed, encompassing parts of eight states. Our people had developed ecological management systems of wildlife and fisheries, along with interstate commerce, government branches with checks and balances, sports arenas, and transportation networks. It was this way for thousands of years.

Then another culture came to Cherokee country, and settlers' disease and law and military conquest soon wiped out most of the Cherokee people. The people of one of the strongest nations in the Western hemisphere were removed from our homelands.

Soldiers and prominent citizens were given land grants for their service in the war against the Cherokee. Their children grew up and divided the land into plots. Many years later, when public education was developed, the new people would look for a place to build their new school, and some farmer would offer a piece of his land. He'd say, "I've got a nice hill in the middle of my cornfield that would be a perfect place for a school."

And there, on the sacred mound, the school would be built. There the children would play and become educated. But they would not be taught much about the people who had lived there for thousands of years. They would learn that Indians of some kind lived around there somewhere, probably out there in the woods. Besides, they were uncivilized people.

What could this society possibly learn from them?

Tread lightly on the soil under your feet. It has a long and significant history.

50

UNRECONCILED KNOWLEDGE

Our treatment of Indians . . . still affects the national conscience. . . . It seems a basic requirement to study the history of our Indian people. Only through this study can we as a nation do what must be done if our treatment of the American Indian is not to be marked down for all time as a national disgrace.

—John F. Kennedy, 1961

Awareness is always a difficult task. We go about our lives taking in information and listening to experiences that align with our own worldviews. We readily accept myths that prop up our perception of ourselves as the "good guys." To disrupt our stability—what social scientists call homeostasis—means to go against our own natural tendencies to be safe and to secure our own future.

When we finally muster the courage to make ourselves aware of the truth, we may find it to be different from our former understanding and difficult to swallow. When we are faced with the dilemma that our opinion does not reconcile with the truth, what do we do? A worldview based on platonic dualism—the Western worldview—equates simple knowledge with experience. In a Western worldview, to know is to do. The problem is that knowing is just partial reality. In other words, to know without doing is a false reality.

As a sort of experiment, I sometimes ask several Native American elders what they believe. The response is always the same: they tell me what they do. There is no space between knowing and doing in an Indigenous worldview; they are the same.

What will we do with the knowledge we gain? How does knowing about injustice change us? How does it change the stories we tell about ourselves and our nation?

If any American touts the ideas of democracy, equality, and inalienable rights—especially if they claim the United States to be a model for the rest of the world—they must deal honestly with real history and with the actions against America's Indigenous peoples. If America is ever to escape from supreme hypocrisy, the claim of freedom for all must deal with the way freedom was taken away from Native Americans.

Unresolved knowledge of injustice is useless unless it is applied in some good way toward those who experienced it.

What action will you take to make others aware of injustices toward Native Americans? How might it actually help those who continue to suffer?

PART SIX

LEARNING THE LIMITS OF PROGRESS

51

GENEROSITY

The white man knows how to make everything, but he does not know how to distribute it. . . . The love of possessions is a disease with them. They take tithes from the poor and weak to support the rich who rule. They claim this mother of ours, the earth, for their own and fence the neighbors away.

—Sitting Bull, Lakota, 1880

When you compare poverty and wealth among the dominant European-based cultures of Canada and the United States to that of Indigenous peoples in North America, you see a wide gap. Both societies base their wealth on what comes from the land, but there are different values concerning the distribution of those resources. Wealth among First Nations people has always come from the abundance of what could be hunted, grown, harvested, and gathered from the abundance of the land. From an Indigenous perspective, that wealth was then considered to be a shared community investment as opposed to an individual asset.

Indigenous people have been able to thrive in what seem the most inhospitable climates and geographies imaginable. This is an amazing fact when you consider the temptation, under such circumstances, to hoard food and resources in order to survive. Yet despite these hardships, Indigenous people in North America have developed values based on generosity, hospitality, and concern for the common good. These Indigenous virtues, nurtured for so long, seem to have sustained Native Americans—assuring not just their survival but their ability to thrive on this continent.

Those raised in Western cultures may have difficulty comprehending the values of hospitality and generosity. The logic behind structures of racism, such as those established by Europeans toward Indigenous Americans, demands that Indigenous people respond likewise, with objectification and violence. This was sometimes but not always the case, especially at first. Yet Indigenous people knew an unseemly response was not a long-term solution, and they knew that it could not be justified by their own values.

To take more than what one needs violates a sense of respect. It takes character to maintain your values in the midst of oppression; it takes courage to open your home or finances to others when you have so little yourself. But these values are worth passing on.

Find someone today with whom you can be generous with your time, wealth, or energy. Who are you teaching to be generous with creation?

52

WHOLE REALITY

You will find something greater in woods than in books. Trees and stones will teach you that which you can never learn from masters.

—Saint Bernard de Clairvaux

We've all heard the term "rose-colored glasses," which means seeing the world as less harsh than it really is. These colored glasses are handed down from generation to generation. Western worldviews hold in common one particular tint—namely, the foundational influence of Platonic dualism, named after the philosopher Plato and handed down from the Greeks. This dualism places more importance on abstract areas of life like our spirit, our soul, or our mind and less importance on physical areas like the Earth or our bodies. You may have heard the saying that someone is so heavenly minded that they're no earthly good. The problem with dualistic thinking is that it separates areas into two, as if reality is no longer whole.

Believe it or not, a whole host of other problems—such as hierarchy, overcategorizing, individualism, patriarchy, racism, religious intolerance, greed, and thinking that says humanity is over nature—flow from dualism. The influence of dualism empowers all these other concerns.

Maybe the best way to combat a bad worldview is to present a better one. Maybe it's enough to know that the Western worldview has been awfully destructive over the last few millennia. And now it is dragging down the whole planet to the point of us all wondering if we will survive the future.

On the other hand, Indigenous worldviews understand all of life as both physical and spiritual, together and inseparable. What difference would it make if we viewed all of life as a whole? What if we understood the Earth itself as our primary spiritual teacher? Then nothing would be without spirit in our understanding. Everything would be understood as related. All life would be sacred. If this were the case, might we be living in a different world today?

We have all been influenced by the sterile and often lifeless Western worldview, thinking certain things are objects, without life or spirit. We all are guilty of understanding certain species in nature as being less important than another—especially less important than us! We have classified and condemned some animals as varmints and some plants as weeds, and yet each has an important role to play in the world. Our worldviews can be changed if we really work on them.

What processes or experiences can you use to challenge your own Western worldview and begin to view life as a whole?

53

DECONSTRUCTING WORLDVIEW

Hearing Mass is the ceremony I most favor during my travels. Church is the only place where someone speaks to me and I do not have to answer back.

—Charles de Gaulle

How does a person begin to deconstruct the way they look at the world? After all, worldviews are deeper than culture and language, although both play a part in shaping our worldview.

Hanging out with those who have a non-Western or Indigenous worldview seems necessary to make changes. Spending time in a situation in which non-Indigenous people are the cultural minority also helps.

To remind us of our intimate connection to creation and to break our dualistic thinking, "action" must become the most important word in Western people's vocabulary. Part of the problem with a Western worldview is that we spend too much time in our own heads, thinking and rethinking, but not enough time acting on our thoughts. To change, we need to embody our thoughts in the world. Spending more time in nature and developing new ways of expressing thanks through outdoor, Earth-honoring ceremonies could be a start.

Through expressing gratitude in ceremony, Indigenous peoples reveal to others and themselves the connection between Creator, human beings, the Earth, and all the rest of creation. A foundation of Native American ceremony is gratitude for the relationships that exist. All indigenous peoples, regardless of what land they inhabited around the world, had their own ceremonies that served a similar purpose.

European people and others can rediscover what their own indigenous ancestors once knew. They can reclaim some of their own indigeneity once again. Whatever your ancestry, discover what symbols and ceremonies, even just the small ones, connected your ancestors to the Earth. Can you incorporate those you find and those you are comfortable with into your own life? Perhaps those you discover, combined with your own land context, can make life more meaningful and more whole for you and others around you.

To move ahead—perhaps simply to survive—we must all be connected to creation in harmony.

What small ceremony can you imagine and perform today that helps you break through to a more Indigenous worldview?

54

PRACTICING RELATIONSHIP

One touch of nature makes the whole world kin.
—William Shakespeare

The Western worldview has had several millennia to develop the hubris necessary to believe every problem can be solved. To its credit, this bizarre way of looking at the world has produced many magnificent products and innovations. The surety of thinking oneself superior in the world has the advantage of breeding extreme confidence. But unfortunately, the Western worldview has not had the foresight to understand its limitations, especially when it comes to nature.

The false sense of control central to the Western worldview is a major problem. It presents itself in economic markets, scientific experiments, and military endeavors. In order to come up with a consistent outcome, the thinking goes, one must have control of the variables.

The problem is that nature, especially weather, is almost completely out of human control.

Consider these facts: The past six years are the hottest on record in twenty-nine countries and Antarctica. CO_2 is being released into the atmosphere faster than any time in the past sixty-six million years. Ice shields are breaking quickly in western Antarctica; without them intact, the melting of two major glaciers will raise sea levels ten feet. One of those glaciers is the size of Florida. A six-foot sea rise would wipe out Miami, Washington, DC, and other major cities.

Climate refugees—those fleeing the effects of the climate crisis, such as hurricanes, tornadoes, wildfires, and flooding—are relocating themselves not just in faraway countries but in places like Louisiana, Florida, California, Oregon, Washington, Indiana, Iowa, and Alaska. More than thirty Alaska towns have had to be relocated because of climate change. To move a town of sixty people costs a million dollars. (Can you multiply?) When sea levels rise, large fish species go extinct, coral reefs die, and topsoil disappears and becomes less healthy. Large mammals and many other species in creation are on the brink of extinction. The air we breathe is becoming more polluted.

How we view nature and how we treat the community of creation has consequences.

We can learn a lesson from Indigenous peoples by understanding our relationship with everything. We are all in this together. Everything that flies, swims, walks, or crawls is our relative.

Discover one practice you can do today that moves your relationship with nature toward intimacy and respect.

55

MARCH OF PROGRESS

What do I think of Western civilization? I think it would be a very good idea.

—Mahatma Gandhi

The Smoky Mountains, including the designated national park boundaries, were once home to the Cherokee Indians. This stunning and beautiful land was the homeland of my people. There were numerous cities (known popularly as "villages") throughout the region for thousands of years. The land was wisely macromanaged and engineered. To ensure the best possible fertility of soil for growing crops, the Cherokee planted in the flood plains by rivers and creeks, allowing the silt left behind to act as fertilizer. They created the optimum grazing conditions for big game like woodland bison, elk, and deer by setting controlled fires to renew the grass each year. They knew how to live with the land so that it would produce the best living conditions for tens of thousands of people without doing permanent damage.

Indigenous people believe we are symbiotically intertwined with the Earth and all her creatures. Each of us—people, frogs, dragonflies, bears, deer, and others—all have a role to play. Each, in some way, depends on the other. "Natural," as I understand it, means having an unbroken ecosystem, one that allows each being to fulfill their reciprocal role to its fullest. Ironically, the idea of "pristine wilderness"—landscapes completely devoid of humans— can exist only in a worldview built upon the dualistic assumption that nature is distinct from human beings. To view a land without humans living with it as being one of harmony? That is actually completely unnatural.

What kind of society sets aside particular places that cannot be exploited while allowing the rest of creation to be raped, com-modified, and brutalized? National parks have been set aside to keep the ones who memorialize them from destroying them! And even then, they bend the laws to extract precious natural resources from these places. The Western "march of progress" just can't help itself from destroying everything Creator has meant for us to sustain.

I am thankful that we have national parks—and I have visited more than a few of them. Yet I have always had a concern that a society with a dualistic worldview, founded primarily upon greed, would eventually exploit these beautiful places as well. Today, this projected fear is now a reality. There is a constant political battle underway to cut timber, drill for oil, and extract minerals from these places of beauty and solace. This desire to despoil some of our last remaining chances to learn from unmolested nature herself seems wholly uncivilized.

To see the future, we need to understand our past. Join or support an organization that is trying to regenerate the Earth.

56

INDIVIDUALISM

Non-cooperation with evil is as much a duty as is cooperation with good.

—Mahatma Gandhi

One of the traits Western humans seem to have laid aside somewhere is cooperation for the good of the group—the common good, as some call it. In our deep, primal selves, we understood that surviving against bad weather, dangerous predators, warring clans, and other unforeseen odds stacked against us meant we needed to look out for each other. To continue our lives, and to ensure survival for generations to come, we knew we had to cooperate.

Usually, a cooperative group meant there was a relationship, of sorts, between the individuals. The relationships and the need for survival bonded these groups together. People often use the word *tribalism* in a negative way, but it needn't be so. In a larger and more superficial sense of cooperative ethos, nationalism is the new tribalism. But one of the problems with nationalism is that it often lacks the richness of true relationship—that, and the fact that national myths are often built of falsehoods and one-sided stories.

In the United States, even nationalism has been superseded by individualism. We might be the most individualistic society in the history of the world. In fact, if the way we treat each other and the rest of the planet is any indication, nationalism is simply a euphemism for selfishness.

The United States makes up about 5 percent of the world's population but uses about 18 percent of the world's energy, mostly from nonrenewable energy sources. We use one-third of the world's paper, a quarter of the world's oil, 23 percent of the world's coal, 27 percent of the world's aluminum, and 19 percent of the world's copper.

Where did we lose that cooperative, communal-oriented, tribal orientation? No matter where we misplaced it, we need to back-track to find it again—and quickly.

With your time and talent and resources, do something generous and cooperative today with others. Repeat the exercise daily.

57

TO BE HUMAN ON EARTH

And forget not that the earth delights to feel your bare feet and the winds long to play with your hair.

—Kahlil Gibran

Pristine is a word people sometimes use to refer to a place that is pure, untouched by human hands, or uncorrupted by so-called civilization. President Theodore Roosevelt set aside the Yellowstone area as a national park, part of a pristine wilderness for the nation to enjoy in perpetuity. Others followed, like the most-visited Great Smoky Mountains National Park and Yosemite National Park, likely the most photographed.

Yet these parks and other demarcated wilderness areas, despite all their grandeur, have never been the "unspoiled wilderness." In fact, the whole idea of a naturally unspoiled wilderness is part and parcel of an American myth. That is based on dualistic thinking that separates people from land, breaking the sacred circle or ecosystem.

One reason Indigenous peoples have been condemned is because we view our relationship with the Earth as very sacred. Indigenous peoples understand our relationship with creation as necessary in order to experience the abundant life Great Spirit intends for us and for all humanity. In other words, to care for creation—to maintain harmony and balance on our lands—is foundationally what it means to be human. If we want to live our lives together in abundance and harmony, and if we want future generations to live this way, we must realize we are all on a journey together to heal our world.

When something is unsustainable, you can be sure it will eventually come to its end. Healing the Earth will take cooperation from all of us.

We must realize that the industrial age has written a check to our world that has insufficient funds. Only a worldview encompassing the interconnectedness between Creator, human beings, and the rest of creation will sustain abundant life.

This work is very spiritual. Such a worldview is fundamentally both Indigenous and human. If we are wise, we will protect creation. This creation is the only one we have been given, and it is central to Creator's investment in us as human beings.

Have you considered the idea that being fully human is the essence of spirituality? Go out and tend Mother Earth in some way today. Feel the sense of spirituality it gives you.

58

PLASTIC SPIRIT

I am just a human being trying to make it in a world that is
rapidly losing its understanding of being human.
—John Trudell, Dakota

A few years ago, I attended a Native American men's retreat in the
land of the Nooksack people. The more familiar way to describe its
location is to say that it was near the border of Washington state
and British Columbia. That pays homage to a mythical nation-
state border, however, and centers both George Washington and
Christopher Columbus. I prefer saying I was in the land of the
Nooksack people, with a view of their sacred mountain in sight.

A Nooksack elder came and spoke to us on the first night.
The elder told us he had just come from a meeting of Nooksack
elders who were all also Nooksack language speakers. In many
tribes, fluent tribal language speakers come together in an effort
to preserve the language. Sometimes they compose words in their
own language to express English words—terms for things or con-
cepts for which the Indigenous language had no words.

The elder addressing us had just come from such a meeting, where they were discussing the word and concept of *plastic*. The elder told us that this group of Nooksack speakers had suggested that plastic might be the only thing on Earth that they understood to have no spirit or life force.

So many plastic bags and bottles have been thrown out to sea that now there exists, in the Pacific Ocean, a whole floating continent made of plastic. Eventually, the plastic breaks down and finds its way into the creatures of the water. In the great cycle of reciprocity, animals and humans eat the seafood, now full of microplastics. As a result of our consumption, they, and we, are full of microplastics.

The small particles of plastic also find their way into the hydrological cycle, becoming rain. Now, even in the most remote areas of Earth, the rain that falls spreads microplastics everywhere: into the soil, into the waters, into all creation.

I wonder if the eventual fulfillment of the Western industrialized worldview is to create a world full of plastic beings. Will that include us—plastic humans who are without spirit or life force?

Wean yourself off plastic. Until you do, reduce your use of it, and recycle what you do use.

59
EXTINCTION

Only when the last tree has died and the last river has been poisoned and the last fish has been caught will we realize we cannot eat money.

—Cree Indian Proverb

As modern humans continue mass extraction of the Earth's resources—water, oil, coal, trees, metals, and minerals—we fail to take seriously the fact that we have reached a tipping point. Humanity should have learned its lessons from the plight of the ivory-billed woodpecker, the woodland bison, and the passenger pigeon. Exploited for too long, those species never recovered. Once they are gone, they are gone forever.

There are limits to progress. There are lines that should never be crossed. But in our modern world, human greed does not take into account such boundaries.

As human beings, we should view every drop of oil, every diamond, every lump of coal, and every source of water with a spiritual eye. We should try seeing our world through the eyes of Great Mystery, from whence it comes.

To continuously take, I think, creates a sickness in us all. To refresh our spirits, we need to create more opportunities to give. We need to remind ourselves that everyone else, and everything else, is just as important as we are.

All the Earth is sacred, as is every life-form inhabiting it. It seems quite foolish that only after we have gone too far will we realize that no amount of capital gains, no extractive economic system, and no modern convenience will be worth the price that we will be forced to pay.

I wonder exactly when modern humanity will drive itself to extinction through greed.

Today, give something away.

60
EARTH RIGHTS

Sooner or later, we will have to recognize that the Earth has rights, too, to live without pollution. What mankind must know is that human beings cannot live without Mother Earth, but the planet can live without humans.

—Evo Morales, Aymara

Yesterday, just down the road from my house, I saw two bags on the side of the road. The bags originated from a fast-food restaurant and were full of someone's trash. We once lived in a southern state where, on a multitude of occasions, my wife and I watched people throw trash out their car windows. Each time we felt a mixture of disgust, anger, and sadness. That's exactly what I felt yesterday.

Now consider the carbon released by combustion engines and the production of concrete, chemicals being dumped in the waterways and aquifers through industries like fracking, and the burying of nuclear waste and toxic sludge. If you're like me, your fury multiplies when you think of these offenses. Yet the root of all these abuses is the same as what drove that person to pitch out the trash on our country road.

Indigenous people's movements around the world have begun to demand that we enact laws, such as those found in Ecuador and Bolivia, to protect the Earth. The law of "Rights of Mother Earth" in Bolivia, as it is sometimes called, grew out of the World People's Conference on Climate Change held in Cochabamba, Bolivia, in 2010. After failed climate talks in Copenhagen prevented the world's Indigenous voices from being heard, proposals for the United Nations' adoption of laws protecting the Earth were presented a year later at the Cochabamba gathering.

Bolivia is struggling to deal with the climate crisis and weather anomalies, such as rising temperatures, melting glaciers, and numerous floods, droughts, and mudslides. Bolivia, like the United States and many other countries, is also a battleground between the rights of Indigenous peoples, especially those who are landless, and the corruption of a corporate state.

In the United States, corporations are protected legally, as persons. But the Earth, which supports them, has no legal rights.

Only a worldview embracing the whole community of creation will sustain the quality of life we all want to enjoy. If we are wise, we will protect the whole community of creation. The fastest way to ensure this happens is by giving the Earth herself rights.

Find out what you can do to establish Earth-rights laws in your community. Here are a few organizations that will help you along the way:

Earth Rights International www.earthrights.org
Eloheh Indigenous Center for Earth Justice www.eloheh
    .org

Earth Justice www.earthjustice.org

Indigenous Environmental Network www.ienearth.org

Earth Rights Institute www.earthrightsinstitute.org

Global Alliance for the Rights of Nature www.therights
ofnature.org

Honor the Earth www.honorearth.org

Soul Fire Farm www.soulfirefarm.org

PART SEVEN

RETURNING TO THE HARMONY WAY

61

HARMONY WAY

I am because of you.

—Desmond Tutu, Xhosa and Tswana

Our Cherokee people have a construct—a way of being—we call *Eloheh*. This lifeway includes our history, culture, law, and all aspects of life. One could say it means "the harmony way," but it is so much more. Eloheh means the ground producing in abundance, the way it should. It means there is no fighting among each other and that everyone is acting as a good relative. Eloheh is knowing the world is in balance, and every being is doing their part. Sometimes it is described also as *Duyukti*: the right road or good path of balance. Eloheh is knowing the importance of community above oneself and your role in it.

Other North American tribes have similar understandings of the harmony way. From my own years of experience among various tribal peoples and my doctoral research, I learned that other tribes also hold a harmony-way concept as a foundation for living. Each tribe has a word or several words in their language that represents living in harmony and balance. In English, some tribes talk about harmony as a way of balance. Some say "beauty way"; others talk of a "good way" or a "good road."

It is safe to assume that other Indigenous peoples around the world have similar understandings of the harmony way. I have known Indigenous people from all around the world who very much relate to this lifeway. This similarity allows some common ground among Indigenous peoples everywhere.

We are all indigenous from somewhere. So what happened? How did the individual become more important than the community? When did competition overtake cooperation? At what point did some civilizations trade knowledge through lived experience and replace its importance with theory?

The answers to these and other important questions are complex. Suffice it to say for now, the way back is through the harmony way of living and being. The way back is through one's relationship with the Earth and the whole community of creation.

Go outside today and hold the soil in your hands. Imagine yourself as just one of the billions of life-forms around you, none more important than the other but each doing its part to maintain harmony and balance.

62

LIKE WATER ON A WINDSHIELD

When we look at what is truly sustainable, the only real model that has worked over long periods of time is the natural world.

—Janine Benyus

Windshield wiper fluid is a great discovery, right? I remember when I first filled the windshield wiper basin of my 1986 Nissan Sentra and then watched as the water hit the windshield and immediately formed little beads. Those beads then rolled off my window and made it clear for me to see while driving in the rain.

Yet this product is one of literally tens of thousands of products destroying our world. I'm not sure what it takes to make windshield wiper fluid. When you go searching for the ingredients, manufacturers make them difficult to find. You find yourself in a world of words and processes you cannot begin to pronounce. Just one of the many dangerous ingredients, methanol, is highly flammable, highly toxic, and is particularly bad for the environment.

But technology, it seems, is progress. That's what we call it anyway. And because we have such products, we carry around attitudes that perpetuate our sense of being more advanced than earlier generations.

Many DIY recipes for making homemade windshield washer fluid exist—and most don't require the use of toxic chemicals. I don't know how well each one works or if there is a trade-off between effectiveness and cost to the environment. But I do know that solutions like these represent real progress.

Why does each generation believe itself to be smarter than the generation that came before? This hubris is compounded when we compare our current "progress" to that of prior centuries and when we believe our technologies are better simply because they are different. Our attitudes are reinforced with every new technology and discovery.

Perhaps technology and discovery are simply ways that we perpetuate our illusions about ourselves and our society. Perhaps discovery is actually *re*discovery, and technology is the compounded sum of our current tools.

We truly believe we are much smarter than the generations and civilizations that came before us. Yet none of those prior generations destroyed the very Earth that feeds them and maintains their existence as a species. No, destroying the planet is the work of today's human beings. Everything in nature screams out, "I want to live and carry on my species!" Yet humans are destroying the very ground upon which we walk, the planet on which our lives depend.

In the meantime, I'll go outside and water my garden. I'll watch the water on my kale and collards form into perfectly small beads—beads that roll off the leaves like water on a windshield.

Modern technology as "discovery" and "progress"? I don't think so. This is something else.

Today, go outside and rediscover one of the inventions of nature.

63

SEEDS

To live without hope is to cease to live.

—Fyodor Dostoevsky

Edith and I have had hundreds and perhaps thousands of people visit us throughout the years. Our time with visitors usually begins with a farm tour, during which we share the joys and heartaches of living with the land. We talk about how we revived a traditional method to accommodate the land or animals. We share the importance of using only open-pollinated seed varieties and some basics about saving your own seeds.

On one of those farm tours, I heard Edith use a phrase that resonated deeply with me. She said, "I believe in the seeds."

I had never heard her say it that way before. She said it with conviction, like an evangelist, completely convinced of the truth: *I believe in the seeds.* Perhaps it sounds stranger to you, reading this, than it did to me that day when I heard her say it. But there is a great lesson contained in this simple truth.

The beauty of seeds still amazes us. These living organisms are planted in the soil by human hands or sometimes by the wind, birds, ants, reptiles, and other creatures. Then seeds are left on their own to create plants, which sometimes grow larger than people. They always work in cooperation with the sun and rain and the temperature, and with microorganisms and fungi and humus. Sometimes they work with just a little cooperation from human beings.

Seeds feed us and give us strength. They shelter us, and give us materials for arts and crafts, and supply the absolute necessities in life.

"Each time I plant them in the ground," my wife says, "I am still surprised and filled with joy when I see them show up and grow." The process of seeds and their growth is truly a daily miracle.

Seeds are sacred, giving life to the planet. I believe in the seeds!

Plant something today, even if just in a pot. Be sure to obtain natural, unadulterated, and unaltered open-pollinated seeds.

64

ADD COFFEE

The most important thing is that each individual must treat all others, all the people who walk on Mother Earth, including every nationality, with kindness. That covers a lot of ground. It doesn't apply only to my people. I must treat everyone I meet the same.

—Tadodaho, Chief Leon Shenandoah, Onondaga

Respect is not a very complex value. Respect means treating everything else in creation as if it matters, as if it is important. When it comes to other humans, to respect someone simply means to treat them the way I would want to be treated if I were in their situation.

Respecting others does not require deep thought. It's simple. I don't want to go without food, so respect calls out to me to feed those who are hungry. I need warmth and shelter from the weather, so respect bids me to find shelter for the houseless. I like to stay clean and have decent-looking clothes on my back, so respect tells me to help provide these for others who need them.

Respect especially applies to those who are different than me. We sometimes spend too much time fearing difference. Yet respect gives me the courage to approach those different from me and to understand their thoughts, ways, and concerns. What I fear in others, they may fear in me.

Fear of the unknown is natural, but it can easily be paralyzing. Rather than allowing our fears to overcome us and coax us into inaction, fear can serve a greater purpose in our lives. Fear can become a catalyst for courage. That sense of fear—of objecting to the idea of coming closer to the unknown—can also light the fuse to our bravery. Fear can move us out of hesitation and into the realm of daring.

Isn't that what I would want others to do for me? I might even like for someone I don't know—someone very different than me, someone who makes me uncomfortable—to surprise me and invite me to share a cup of coffee or a meal. As we sip our coffee or eat our food, we would actually listen to each other. Now that's respect!

Listen to someone you don't understand today. If possible, add coffee.

65

THE LANGUAGE OF BASKETS

In Silence there is eloquence. Stop weaving and see how the pattern improves.

—Rumi

Baskets have their own language. Even though I don't speak it, I try to understand them just the same.

Edith and I have a great assortment of Indian baskets. We did not set out to be basket collectors; it's just that in Indian country, baskets are a common gift. Each tribe has a slightly different process and style and often different materials that go into making the basket. As I have watched Indigenous women weave baskets, I observe slight smiles of great pleasure. Their facial expressions reveal their connection to their teachers and their ancestors, who have done the same thing for hundreds and even thousands of years. A lot is revealed about our cultures through our baskets and even through how they are made.

I have only made Cherokee baskets, which seems appropriate given that is my ancestry. Much of our history and culture is demonstrated in the weave. When you begin a Cherokee basket, you start with a particular cross-pattern that reveals our sacred fire: our religion and spirituality, so to speak. The pattern continues until it includes the sacred water: the rivers that provide the water for our ceremonies and the place where we always made our homes, in the fertile valleys alongside rivers and streams. The weaving continues until it ends with the mountains: our homeland, underneath which everything else in the basket sits. Those mountains stand guard, protecting us and providing for our people.

My general understanding of baskets and my description of them here do not compare with the wisdom of our traditional basket-makers. If I wanted to pursue this craft, I would have much to learn. In the meantime, baskets are displayed in every room of our house. Some hang on walls. Others function much like they were meant to be used: for holding items or collecting food when we go out berry-picking. Baskets, you see, were originally made to be functional.

I don't know the story of each basket we own. The tribal traditions were not given to us—just the baskets. But I do know each has its own culture and its own story. Each basket represents love from the basket-maker. So I give thought to every basket. And out of respect, each spring, all our baskets are given new life through a bath of spring water. As with all things Indigenous, every basket has its own way of speaking, even if I don't understand the language.

What is the meaning of the crafts and decorations in your own home? What do they communicate?

66

THE JOY OF WILD-TENDING

Before I started writing about food, my focus was really on the human relationship to plants. Not only do plants nourish us bodily—they nourish us psychologically.

—Michael Pollan

What a thrill it is to have someone who really knows about the plants on your land take the time to point them out to you. It's like finding treasure right underneath your nose! I have been fortunate enough to have this happen on numerous occasions. Several times I have been joined by experienced wild-tenders who walk along on the land with me, grazing on certain plants, pointing out the medicinal properties of others. The joy of discovery of my plant relatives makes me happy. Just knowing they are there brings a deep sense of peace.

Wild-tending is just one of numerous ecological preservation movements across the land. Wild-tending, a relatively small movement that uses deep understanding of plant and animal life to tend to the land, is of great importance. The Indigenous people of the land are the original wild-tenders. Everything from deer to plants to the use of water was carefully kept in balance so there would be enough left to sustain them in the future and for generations to come.

A wild-tending worldview—one that maintains a careful watch on the whole community of creation, assuring everything stays in balance for generations to come—was born through centuries of trial and error. I'm certain that in the earliest days of their learning, the host peoples of the land paid a price to learn those hard lessons. The reason I am so certain about these facts is because many of our tribes have stories of an earlier time—a time during which things were out of balance ecologically. Those stories attribute the imbalance to human greed.

Two of my friends are serious wild-tenders. Their commitment to restoring nearly extinct species inspires me to do the same. Most often, their work is unknown to anyone else. They identify places where native species have either gone extinct or are near extinction. Then, without financial or moral support and without accolades, they go about replanting seeds and plants in those areas. When possible, they involve the local tribes in the area. That way, the relationship between the people of the land, the land, and those plants is reestablished.

My two friends are not Native Americans. They simply know to do what is right, so they do it.

Research native plants in your area. Which ones are barely surviving that you could help to restore? While you are at it, research the tribal people of your land and their relationship with those plants. Who knows what may come of it?

67

TOLERANCE

In the practice of tolerance, one's enemy is the best teacher.

—Dalai Lama

One of the pitfalls of the Western worldview is intolerance for ideas and people different from itself. I have developed a long theoretical formula that I think explains Western intolerance. I won't bore you with the details. For now, suffice it to say that since the days of Greece and Rome, the West has seen itself as the highest form of civilization on Earth. Members of Western civilization have so normalized and universalized that understanding of themselves that societies that don't share those same principles are seen as suspect, if not primitive or savage.

In precontact Native America, tolerance became a strong virtue. Sure, members of one tribe may have thought themselves superior to members of another tribe; of this there is no doubt. But there remained a belief that what was best for one people could be different from what was best for others. Each people group was free to choose their own ways as they understood them. In other words, "You do your thing, and we'll do ours."

In all my studies, and in all the stories I have heard from elders, I have not found a single war fought among America's original people that concerned one group trying to convert another to a particular religion or culture. This historical truth stands in direct contrast to Western civilizations, which have engaged in an almost constant stream of wars over religion and nationhood.

When it comes down to it, can we really force our beliefs on another person without disrespecting their personhood, their right to choose?

Has arguing about beliefs caused a strain on one of your relationships with a loved one? If so, what could you do today to loosen the grip of the argument on your mind and on the relationship?

68

RESPECT FOR ELDERS

Morality comes with the sad wisdom of age, when the sense of curiosity has withered.

—Graham Greene, Oneida

One of the most difficult things for outsiders to do when entering Indian country is to listen. When someone blatantly disrespects an elder, it disrupts the order of things. Elders are considered a gift to the community, not to be abused or disrespected in any way. If an elder takes the time to lend their wisdom to a situation, we listen without interruption—no matter how long they talk.

Elders have lived long lives, and they remember the old ways. Elders have seen a lot more than most of us have, and we believe that listening to and learning from their wisdom can save us from future pain and disaster. We believe they are approaching the crossover time, when they will walk on to the other world and come closer to Great Mystery. All of these beliefs and more create a special place for elders among Native Americans.

I was taught that if I want to ask an elder for help in some way, I need to offer a gift to the elder. I have done this on many, many occasions. Sometimes the gift has been a sacred plant like tobacco. Other times I have given them some fruit. Still other times, on special occasions, I've given a whole "elder basket," which includes flour and coffee and sugar and other items such as handkerchiefs, tobacco, a flashlight, and clothes hangers.

These needful items are always given freely, without expectation of anything in return. If the elder chooses to accept the gift, they usually respond in a helpful way, with words of wisdom or the advice that I am seeking. But I can't presume they will. If I did, their words would not be a gift but rather a trade. And there's a difference.

Without a doubt, the most meaningful wisdom I have received throughout my life came from my time listening to elders. They don't want us to make a big deal over them. Many don't even like to volunteer their status as an elder, and they defer to the elders who lived before them. But we can remember the elders with a small gift. Simply listening to them is enough.

Give a gift to an elder in your life today. Move a box for them, cut firewood, or deliver a basket of fruit, and then listen to them. You might be surprised what happens next.

69

SOLVING MODERN PROBLEMS

We are the conscience of your technology. We are the human-
izers of your institutions. We matter, quite apart from your
recognition of our worth. . . . We are a threat to entrenched
powers-that-be who refuse to open the doors of opportunity and
choice to all. We are a challenge to the mindset of greed. . . . We
are good medicine for you.

—Adrian Jacobs, Ganosono, Cayuga

I read about a conflict regarding a highway project being planned
for an Indian reservation in Montana. The state insisted that the
highway go directly through the reservation in order to save
the (non-Native) taxpayers money. Many of the people on the reservation were against it. They understood that it would endanger
much of the wildlife that needed to cross the reservation on trails
they had established over generations.

The state wouldn't budge—at first. The norm in this type of
conflict is for the tribe, in order to have a say, to sue the state,
which is usually backed by large corporate interests. This story
took a different turn, however. According to the article I read, the

state agreed to create a sort of tunnel system under the highway where animals often crossed. That way large and small wildlife could still cross the land on their known trails.

I don't know the details, but I can imagine that this solution came from one of the wise elders of the tribe. It has all the markings of an Indigenous conscience, a Native way of problem-solving.

I don't know how this plan turned out for the tribe or for the bears, elk, moose, deer, and other animals. I hope that, by the state's choice to listen to the wisdom of the Indigenous people, better relationships were established between all the people involved. I especially hope that many animal lives were saved—animals who might have otherwise been killed on the highway. Undoubtedly, as with any modern mechanism such as a highway, the lives of some animals, and perhaps even the lives of some people, were lost.

We live in a crazy, fast-paced, technological world. Too much technology has been and continues to be developed without concern for the community of creation. Shouldn't we listen to the wisdom of the people who have lived on the land for tens of thousands of years? Before we unleash the often-destructive elements of modernity on the world, shouldn't we know the costs to the whole community of creation?

What Indigenous values and wisdom can you apply to one of the modern inventions that you use?

70

HOSPITALITY

The hospitality of the wigwam is only limited by the institution of war.

—Charles Eastman, Ohiyesa, Dakota

My wife and I are often asked what we do at Eloheh Indigenous Center for Earth Justice and Eloheh Farm. Based on our years of experience, we know what people are generally asking with that particular question. They want to know what programs we have employed. They want to be shown where we practice our farming or where we hold our classes. Sometimes what they are really asking about is our curriculum.

We usually laugh to ourselves when we hear the question because we think what we offer is, simply put, hospitality.

Both Edith and I come from families and homes in which hospitality was the rule. During both our childhoods, we shared our parents' homes with multiple cousins, aunties and uncles, nieces and nephews, and others. Sometimes I had to vacate my own bed for several weeks at a time so a visitor would have a soft place to land.

During my relatives' "visits"—which often lasted weeks or even months—my parents would lay out a pallet of blankets and quilts on the floor in the living room. There on the floor, six or eight of us kids would all sleep together. I recall these as fun and exciting times. After tucking us all in, the adults would have to come back in the room several times to quiet us from our talking and laughter. Today, all I can think about is how uncomfortable it must have been to sleep on the floor. But I suppose children's young bones are made to withstand hard floors, especially when enduring it with others.

Since my wife and I have been married—which is now more than thirty years—our home has been a constant place of hospitality to friends, family, and strangers. Their stays have lasted from hours to months. Sometimes people tell us that we have the gift of hospitality, but I'm not sure I would call it that. I don't think there is any special skill or magic to it.

Each visit is different, and each visitor's needs vary. We simply try to be good hosts. Maybe that's the magic.

Be a good host to someone today.

PART EIGHT

LOVING EARTH

71

FIRST MEDICINE

Because no matter who we are or where we come from, we're all entitled to the basic human rights of clean air to breathe, clean water to drink, and healthy land to call home.

—Martin Luther King III

In Minnesota, a group of women take their sacred duty to protect the water seriously. They are the Anishinabe Water Protectors. These women, young and old, walk the shores of lakes and rivers, praying through ceremony for the protection of the Earth's sacred water, which is the Earth's blood. It seems only right that women, who consist of more water than men and who are more physically reactive to the moon that governs the tides and other waters, would be on the front lines in protecting the waters.

Our traditional North American Indigenous people often refer to water as "the first medicine." Water is the Earth's most precious resource, and it is necessary for all life to survive. It is in and around everything. We need it.

Water in Cherokee tradition—and every other Indigenous tradition I know—is considered sacred. What do I mean by *sacred*? I mean every ocean, every lake, every bog and slew and estuary, every creek, every waterfall, every spring, and even the rain—perhaps especially the rain—are considered gifts from Great Mystery.

Many American Indigenous peoples have ceremonies that involve water or that reference water. The ceremonies almost always, if not always, involve deep appreciation for water and the life it brings. Whether it comes from rain, or springs, or rivers, or oceans, there is much gratitude expressed by Native Americans, all across this land, for water.

Perhaps this is true of all peoples, including Western Europeans. I think that many of the European tribes also understood water's sacredness at one point in their history. (After all, we are all indigenous from somewhere.) I also think their descendants have largely forgotten just how important and just how sacred water is.

Begin reading literature, both fiction and nonfiction, poetry and story, about the importance of water. If possible, research water from various traditions. Look for the sacred connection to water, and then find ways to protect it.

72

SPRINGS

Beauty is eternity gazing at itself in a mirror.

—Khalil Gibran

I've been told a number of times that springs were sacred to my Kee-toowah ancestors. But no one had to tell me that for me to believe it.

Lots of stories explain why springs are sacred. I suppose those stories are good to know and learn from. The stories are sacred in their own right. But to me, springs can speak for themselves. Everything around a spring commands me to be still: to listen and observe the sacred moment I am sharing with the soil, and trees, and bugs. The shining sun and bright sky in the day, and the glowing moon and twinkling stars at night, all frame the hallowed experience.

Of all the springs that I have enjoyed spending time with, none compare to my sacred Blue Hole. Oh, I don't claim to own it. Hundreds—well, honestly, thousands—before me have likely felt the same personal feelings about *their* Blue Hole.

I will say that it is located in Cherokee country, but I won't say more. To speak of it as a tourist spot would betray the unspoken vows that I make each time I visit. When I am in that area of the country, a visit to the Blue Hole has become a regular pilgrimage.

When my children were small, we lived only a few hours from the Blue Hole. As a family, we would take the children there to conduct our going-to-water ceremony. I would also take a little of the spring's water home, after asking her permission, for special use in ceremonies requiring spring water. And though I hated to capture a part of such a blessed body of pure water, releasing her later for ceremonial purposes made me happy. She could still continue the never-ending cycle of water's natural purpose and course; I had simply borrowed a portion of her essence for a very brief moment in an eternity of time. Springs have taught me many things, including patience.

On the other side of sacred springs is supposed to be another dimension: a world where everything is like this one but in complete harmony and balance. Springs also remind me to live in *this* world in the good way I am living in the other.

Do you have a sacred place to go and reflect on life? Be sure you do, and visit it often.

73

COOPERATION

Strictly speaking, one never "keeps" bees—one comes to terms with their wild nature.

—Sue Hubbell

There is an old Cherokee story about how disease and medicine came into the world. The whole story is much longer than I could share here. But in brief, it goes like this:

There was a time when the people began to kill all the animal people wantonly, without regard for harmony and balance. This included the four-legged animal people, the winged animal people, the swimming animal people, and the crawling animal people. The animals decided they had had enough, so they came together in a great council. There they decided they would seek revenge on the humans for their disrespectful actions.

The bears took charge of the meeting first. They asked, "How are the people killing us?" "With bows and arrows," some of the animals replied. "Then we will take revenge with bows and arrows," said the bears. After hard work, the bears were able to construct bows and arrows; but their claws kept getting in the way, making them unsuitable archers.

So the animals decided the grubworm would lead the rest of the council to find a solution to the problem. After the grubworm had solicited all the other animals' input, he came up with the idea to put diseases on the people. And so they did. The animal council sent to the humans many diseases: chicken pox, smallpox, measles, mumps, and various influenzas. And the people began to succumb to these diseases. First the infants and children, and then the elders, and finally everyone was dying from the revenge of the animals. The people went to the animals and asked for forgiveness, but the animals would not relent.

All the while, the plant people had been observing what was happening. They held their own council, and they decided the people had learned their lesson. Out of compassion for the humans, the plants began to send cures to various human people's dreams. In those dreams, they showed the humans exactly how to use plants for healing each disease. Soon the people recovered, and the animals, the plants, and the humans held a council together.

In that council, they all decided that every hunter must pray the night before the hunt, sending a message to the animal, and only an animal who presents itself freely to the hunter could be taken. Then the hunter must offer tobacco to the Earth, to the animal, and to Great Mystery, giving thanks for the food provided for his family. Every usable part of the carcass must be employed.

If this practice continued, the animals would stop spreading disease. Since disease was already in the world, the plants would continue to send cures in the humans' dreams. But every time a plant is taken, tobacco would again be offered. Eventually, harmony and balance would again be restored to the Earth.

The success of our time on Earth depends on your cooperation with all the rest of creation. How might you restore balance in your own community today?

74

FIVE HUNDRED YEARS

If we pollute the air, water and soil that keep us alive and well, and destroy the biodiversity that allows natural systems to function, no amount of money will save us.

—David Suzuki

I have an Indigenous friend who is a professor and an expert on the Mayan calendar system. The Mayan calendar predates the Gregorian calendar, which is in wider use today. According to some experts, the Mayan calendar is more accurate.

While popular belief held that the Mayan calendar had predicted the end of the world on December 21, 2012, my friend showed me that the actual date was 2013. And she clarified that although the calendar suggested that chaos and imbalance would reign, it wasn't signifying the end of the world. Rather, the Mayans issued a dire warning that we have just a few short years to bring the world back into harmony and balance where peace reigns. The alternative is perpetual pandemonium.

One might look at the world right now and wonder if we have crossed over into the age of the apocalypse. Leaders around the world move toward fascism and promote violence. Pandemics take millions of lives. Wildfires, hurricanes, tornadoes, floods, droughts, and record-breaking temperatures increase. Rather than thinking all this is occurring through happenstance, I suggest that these are the natural consequences of human actions taken over centuries.

If we could look at Western Europe as it was about five hundred years ago, we could observe many of the phenomena we are experiencing today. Hardwood forests were being depleted to make castles, cathedrals, and fortresses, and to fuel fires hot enough to forge iron tools and weapons. The bays and rivers were overfished and polluted. Disease was rampant. Water was largely undrinkable.

When comparing the problems of Europe five hundred years ago to America now, there are striking similarities. We should ask ourselves, "What is the common thread between then and now?"

What caused the world to spin out of balance then is the same culprit that is causing our current disarray—namely, the Western worldview. Western civilization has developed a mechanistic view of nature that is nonrelational, competitive, and based on imperial expansion. After more than five hundred years, you'd think Western society would have learned the lessons the Earth had to teach.

We only have one Earth. We may only have a few years left to learn a different way of thinking and living. The Mayans were telling us nothing new. Indigenous people have learned, through millennia of observation, trial, and error, a healthy way to live with each other on the Earth without destroying it. I think the Mayans were right.

The best way to think differently is to immerse oneself in the culture and wisdom of those from whom you wish to learn. Chart a learning plan today.

75

ENERGY AND
THE FOOD CHAIN

There is an urgent need to stop subsidizing the fossil fuel indus-
try, dramatically reduce wasted energy, and significantly shift
our power supplies from oil, coal, and natural gas to wind,
solar, geothermal, and other renewable energy sources.

—Bill McKibben

When we think about energy according to the first two laws of
thermodynamics, we remember that energy can neither be created
nor destroyed. It can only change forms. The total energy of the
universe remains the same.

We know, too, about entropy: a state of randomness or disorder.
We know that the entropy of an isolated system that is not in equi-
librium (balance) tends to increase over time. In other words, disorder, in a closed system, always increases. I'm no Bill Nye the
Science Guy, but I have learned enough to know that isolated
systems—those not in harmony with the rest—are not headed to
a happy place.

In the big picture, where do you think most of the Earth's energy is stored? You may have guessed it already: phytoplankton. Yes, microscopic creatures in the world's oceans are where and how the Earth invests in most of her energy. Phytoplankton supply as much photosynthesis as all the world's plant life! In other words, microscopic creatures of the sea give us the gift of breath. They also form the foundation of the food web of all our oceans, making most other ocean life possible. Unfortunately, phytoplankton are fast declining due to human thoughtlessness.

Knowing that energy is part of a whole system and that it must go somewhere, who do you think is the largest consumer of phytoplankton? The answer is in the question: zooplankton! Again, strange little creatures found in the world's oceans are the answer; zooplankton are the number one consumer of the world's energy. In exchange, they supply half the world's oxygen! Beyond the great plankton energy cycle are secondary consumers like fish, whales, insects, and microorganisms like bacteria and algae. Most mammals, including humans, are not very far up the energy cycle scale. But we are tertiary consumers. Like a goat grazing here and nibbling there, we simply pick up the leftover energy in the world. This is the way it should be, as nature has ordered it.

Unfortunately, humans have begun to move up the scale by consuming more than our share of the Earth's energy. Through industrial-scaled extraction of petroleum and minerals, and through depletion of forest and topsoil, humankind has crossed a boundary we were never meant to cross. And Mother Earth does not like it. Because of human hubris, we are taking more than our fair share of the Earth's energy.

To restore harmony, the Earth is forced to attack the presumed primary consumers, temporarily moving herself to the top of the food chain. If we don't stop our imbalanced consumption, she will be forced to consume us. Tertiary consumers may be expendable—

phytoplankton are not. And it's not that the Earth is a monster; it's just that she was made to survive.

Find ten ways you can renew, reuse, and recycle in order to lower your own consumption of the Earth's energy. Here are two of many websites to get you started:

Conserve Energy Future https://tinyurl.com/3s6nb5w4
US Environmental Protection Agency www.epa.gov/recycle/reducing-and-reusing-basics

76

HEALTHY SOIL,
HEALTHY EARTH

Once we have action, hope is everywhere.

—Greta Thunberg

The world is in a mess. With so much going wrong, it is difficult to find hope for our future.

People put more than ninety million tons of toxic pesticides and fertilizers on American lawns each year. Most of what Americans call weeds are actually food or medicine. Most of those pesky insects are actually beneficial to our immediate environment. Nature has sent us helpers . . . and we kill them.

The faster, bigger, cheaper approach to our food systems is also draining the Earth's resources dry and destroying our health. The Earth's soil is being depleted at thirteen times the rate it can be replaced.

In the last century, we have lost 75 percent of our crop varieties. Over the past decade, we've dumped one hundred million tons of herbicides onto our crops, polluting our soil and streams. Genetically engineered crops are completely altering the composition of soil bacteria in the fields where such crops are grown. We have lost our relationship with food and food workers.

These are just a few of the facts haunting us every day. Here are some practical suggestions for reversing those trends:

- Grow food in your yard. Or simply rewild your space by just letting your lawn grow naturally into a meadow.
- Shop as much as possible in ways that support local, farm-direct, in-season growing. Look for produce grown from seeds that are open-pollinated and non-GMO and that has not been sprayed with insecticides or herbicides.
- Grow your own vegetables from open-pollinated, non-GMO seeds. Save your seeds.
- Learn how to compost to build up the soil. You can use red worms too!
- Shop at farmers' markets, or join a CSA group (Community Supported Agriculture) or farmer's coop.
- Learn how to preserve your own food (freeze, can, smoke, dry).
- Stay away from most packaged food—in other words, anything your great-grandparents wouldn't recognize.
- Save water, don't waste it. As much as possible, catch it, store it, and drip it.
- Attract pollinators—bees, hummingbirds, and butterflies—with wildflowers.
- Soak, scrub, and wash nonorganic fruits and vegetables.

Promote biodiversity everywhere. When we take action on behalf of sacred Earth, hope is not far from any one of us!

Healthy soil means a healthy Earth and healthy creatures—and hope! What ideas from the list above sound doable in your life?

77

VIOLETS

No matter how chaotic it is, wildflowers will still spring up in the middle of nowhere.

—Sheryl Crow

In the spring and early summer, the fields around our house are replete with beautiful little flowers. The flowers of the American violet are tiny compared to what most people think of when they think of violets: the African violet. The American violets adorn themselves in yellow, white, and shades of—wait for it—violet. Fields of purple and yellow and white violets paint a masterpiece for the eye. These longtime native American violets are healing plants, offering food, medicine, and beauty to creatures in a perfectly timed manner.

All parts of the violet—the flowers; the heart-shaped, waxy leaves with ruffled edges; and the stems—have been used medicinally for generations, as breathing aids and for women's health issues. They also look and taste great in salads. (Note, however, that the African violet should not be ingested.)

The American violet plant is self-propagating, stemming from a rhizome root and miniscule seeds held tight in little pods that resemble boney fingers until they are ready to be released in the late fall. The tiny seeds are covered with fats and sugars that are undetectable to the naked eye.

Interestingly enough, at the very same time the American violet drops its seeds, insects like slugs and ants are storing up fats and sugars for the coming winter. The seeds are carried hither and yon by the crawling gourmets, who consume the outer layer of the seeds and then discard them. The seeds stratify and start another rhizome. Then in the spring, another field adorns itself with food, medicine, and beauty.

This is the way of nature: cooperative, reciprocal, harmonious.

We are happy. The ants and slugs are happy. And the American violet is happy to perform its annual ceremony.

Begin to identify the plants in your community. Can you learn enough about them to begin identifying their annual ceremony?

78

THE DEER PEOPLE

You have to leave the city of your comfort and go into the wilderness of your intuition. What you'll discover will be wonderful. What you'll discover is yourself.

—Alan Alda

We live a few miles from town and along a gravel road, practically unseen by our neighbors. We often see a little family of black-tail deer around the property, much of which is wooded. I was surprised yesterday when a relatively young doe walked casually down our driveway and to within ten feet of the house, undisturbed by one of our cats, who was following in curiosity. Usually, the deer people keep at least a fifty-yard distance from us. This was an unusual and beautiful break in my day.

Cherokee people have many tales of Awi' or Kawi', depending on the dialect one employs. These stories speak of our covenant with the deer people. A hunter must sing and pray before setting out, asking permission of the deer people to supply food for one's family. If Awi' does not present himself as a sacrifice, no shots can be taken. If the hunter does not put tobacco on the ground to show deep gratitude after the sacrifice, Awi' Yonega, the little white deer spirit, has the right to curse the hunter with arthritis. Beyond such agreements, a hunter must use all the parts and let nothing go to waste.

These stories are cautionary tales, and they speak to a relationship with the deer people. The stories speak of balance with nature, and they also tell of the character of the deer people. They are generous and kind—but do not cross them.

At some critical times in my life, the deer people have helped me make decisions. In one particularly stressful time, as I sought to determine my future path, I found myself in deep turmoil. At the time, I was building a house in the Florida panhandle with my dad. We had been there from January to April, and I was struggling daily with my sense of life's work. What direction should my life take? Should I choose a career serving people or one that secures my financial future?

One night I fought myself nearly all night long over that decision, and I finally found peace when I asked for a sign from the deer people. Up to that point in our stay, we had not seen even one deer. But the next morning, on our way to the job site, just before we turned in the driveway, seven deer crossed in front of our truck.

Over a decade later, I was agonizing for direction once again. I was sitting in a tiny meadow in the woods of Wisconsin, desperately seeking discernment, when a spotted fawn came within twenty feet of me and just laid down. She looked at me for perhaps ten or twenty minutes. Time is often hard to discern during sacred moments. In what seemed to be a soft version of a stare-down contest, we kept looking into each other's eyes. In the most sacred stillness, I discerned the voice of all the ages speaking words that reaffirmed the earlier decision I had made so long ago, the one that changed my life direction.

Have you ever looked to nature for an answer to an important, even life-changing decision? When you come to a critical decision next in your life, look to what is natural.

79

HEART DESIRES

It is always with excitement that I wake up in the morning wondering what my intuition will toss up to me, like gifts from the sea. I work with it and rely on it. It's my partner.

—Jonas Salk

My family and I spent seven years serving the Indigenous communities of northern Nevada. Much of our lives have been given to tribal peoples who are different from ourselves. To become a good relative requires learning the host people's ways and learning to hold those ways as gifts that are as precious as your own ways. In all our years of encountering various Indigenous cultures, we have tried our best to be good relatives.

One fall day, I felt something inside gnawing at me, but I couldn't figure out just what it was. I had a very unsettled spirit. So I grabbed my rattle and headed down to a small creek. As I sat there by a small pondlike feature in the creek, across from the only tree in sight, I began to understand what was bothering me.

I had learned songs from so many other tribal backgrounds, singing with both the big drum and hand drum. In dreams, I had even been given a few songs in other languages. But I had never been given a song in my own language. I'm not a Cherokee speaker. On a couple of occasions, I had attempted to learn our language. One time, while living in eastern Oklahoma, I had learned enough that I'd actually made it to the basics of Cherokee speech—the equivalent of what a Cherokee toddler might know. But when a language isn't lived out daily, it becomes dormant.

I began to realize I was sad that I had never been given a song in my own people's language. As I sat there across from that tree, a songbird landed in its lower branches. Another landed, and then another, until there were six or seven small birds in the tree.

As I listened to the birds, I began to hear a song in my own head. *"Unethlanahi yowegi"* came to me, over and over again. Then more words came, all in Cherokee. Before I knew it, I found myself singing this song, in my ancestors' language, aloud, with my rattle bringing a full accompaniment.

To my surprise, the birds didn't fly away. More came. As I kept singing the song, over and over again, I was also watching the birds. A larger woodpecker joined the smaller birds on that tree, and a hawk landed on the higher branches, and none of the smaller birds flew away.

I have no idea how long I had been sitting there singing when a duck landed on the creek. I somehow knew that if I stopped singing, they would all fly away. So I kept singing, for what seemed like an hour.

Finally, my voice gave out and I could sing no longer. As if on cue, the birds all flew away.

Take time to understand the desires of your own heart when you feel them. Seek the answers in nature.

80

SPEAKING HEARTS

No notes. You speak from deep in your heart. It's easy.
—Manny "Pacman" Pacquiao

One of my wife's distant relatives was Chief Washakie. Washakie was chief of the Eastern Shoshones for many years, and he lived to be over a hundred years old. He is said to have been a striking figure: dark, with shining silver hair, a genetic trait that my wife also displays. He was also known to have been a brave warrior in battle.

The story goes that the president of the United States was awarding Washakie a great gift for his service as an ally in the campaign against the Sioux. The gift was a silver saddle. The president's aides had accompanied the saddle all the way to Wyoming, and the press was there, ready to report the old chief's reaction to the gift. But after the saddle was presented to him, Washakie said nothing. The spokesperson for the president asked Washakie to comment on this beautiful silver saddle.

Still, Washakie stood in solemn silence.

Again, the man from Washington pressed the chief for a response. "Don't you want to send a message back to the Great White Father in Washington, DC?" he asked.

Yet Washakie never moved his lips.

The press and government officials alike were steaming in their indignance. "How dare this old Indian slight the president this way!" they mumbled. So one more time they all began to solicit Washakie for a response.

Finally, the uncomfortable silence was broken. Washakie slowly moved his way to the center of the platform and opened his mouth. This is what he said: "The White man thinks with his mind, and he has many words to describe his thoughts. The Indian thinks with his heart, and the heart has no words."

Today you have the opportunity to think with your heart. Experiment with choosing silence sometime today.

PART NINE

LOVING SPIRIT

81
THE DIRECTIONS

Religion is for people who are scared to go to hell. Spirituality is for people who have already been there.

—Bonnie Raitt

I was taught not to talk too much about myself. I was told we are supposed to let others say good things about us but not to say them ourselves. It still always bothers me when, during a podcast interview or public presentation, the person in charge tells me to introduce myself by letting everyone know what I do. I suppose that's the American way, but it's not my way. I'd hope that my invitation to speak came as a result of my own merits. But if the person interviewing me doesn't even know enough about me to introduce me, then I wonder why I was asked to speak in the first place. And that troubles me indeed!

As a child in Sunday school, when I was first taught to pray, I was told to fold my hands, bow my head, and close my eyes. Later in life, I learned to pray with my eyes open and by facing the seven directions: east, south, west, north, sky, Earth, and then, for myself. I like the open-eyed, seven directions prayer much better.

So I face the east, remembering to be thankful for the new day and all new things that come. Then I turn to the south, where the warm sun provides time to work and take care of life's necessities. I turn to the west, where the sun sets, accepting the places of death and darkness, which are all part of life. Then I face to the north: toward winter, innovation, storytelling, and the passing on of traditions and the building of family.

I turn back to the east and look up, thanking Great Mystery for all things in life. Then I look down, to show my gratitude to Mother Earth, from where all things grow. Finally, my last thought is of myself. I ask for help because I am simply a human being.

Having first recognized everything else around me, I better understand my near unimportance. I am just a simple man standing in a great world. To be standing on this Earth is a gift. Everything around me is real. Everything is spirit-filled. I am fully and physically present, but even more, I am spirit.

Take time today to find comfort in your smallness, and let prayer remind you of your place on sacred Earth.

82

LIFE, DEATH, AND NOW

This religion does not teach me to concern myself of the life that shall be after this, but it does teach me to be concerned with what my everyday life should be.

—Redbird Smith, Keetoowah

There is something life-giving about being out in nature. I don't think the sense of renewal comes just from seeing new life and new growth, either, although spring gives us a superdose of that feeling. Even in the winter chill, however—on a walk through cold snow, or a moment on the porch on a bleak and weary winter day—our spirits are somehow refreshed.

In the winter, death is everywhere. Leaves have withered and fallen from the deciduous trees. Animals are hidden or hibernate. Birdsongs of joy that one hears in the spring are largely absent; but the shrill cry of a hawk, a winged doomsday for small rodents, becomes even more clear.

The fall season prepares us for death and decay, and winter doses it out in great measure. Still, I love the silent still of winter's death chant.

Death is simply another part of living. Because death is truly sad, we don't like to think about it. But death is our reality and life continues after that.

Perhaps winter is meant to remind us that life is bigger than ourselves. Perhaps we should think more often about the smallness of our existence compared to the greatness of the world.

That way, when we contribute even the smallest act of kindness in the world around us—whether the receiver be human or nonhuman—we can see just how very important and preciously natural that one act of kindness becomes.

May the reminder of death today allow you to see the bigger picture. How might reflecting on death move you to at least one act of kindness?

83

AN EAGLE

Life is one big road with lots of signs.

—Bob Marley

Years ago, one Sunday afternoon, our family had lunch with a group of Christian men from Indiana outside, in the courtyard of our church. I told them the story of a time that four eagles guided me while I put together a ceremony. They didn't understand that very well, so I explained that sometimes Creator sends eagles or hawks or other birds as good messengers. Sometimes an eagle or a hawk can confirm the direction we are taking in life or perhaps even give us a message to go another way.

I could tell they were not putting much stock into what seemed to them to be some kind of pagan superstition. One of the men stood up, walked to the end of the picnic table, and said what the rest of the men were likely thinking: "I can't really buy into your understanding of God working through eagles and such." I could tell that he intended his statement as a defense of his faith. I think he was concerned that I might be leading the group astray.

After his proclamation, there was an awkward moment in which no one said anything. Suddenly, before anyone could say a word to relieve the pregnant silence, a golden eagle appeared in the sky. Flying over the roof from the other side of the building, the massive eagle swooped within about ten feet of the head of the man who had just spoken. He actually ducked because the eagle was just that close. We watched as the eagle turned and rose once again into the sky.

Astonished by what we had just witnessed, we all just sat there for a moment. The intense silence continued as we all looked at him. Finally the man spoke: "Well, that was just a coincidence."

I am always disappointed that Western people have so much difficulty understanding how Great Mystery speaks and acts through the nonhuman parts of the community of creation. Captivated by their own enlightenment-bound thinking, some people cannot conceive of Creator speaking through a bird or an animal. To them, it is nonrational and seemingly out of spiritual bounds.

Yet for Indigenous peoples, creation is the primary teacher. To many Indigenous thinkers, Great Mystery is expressed in and through creation in a personal way. Why wouldn't a Golden Eagle guide us?

Whatever your conception of Great Mystery, make a connection with that force or being when outside today.

84

RELIGION AND SPIRITUALITY

I prayed for twenty years but received no answer until I prayed with my legs.

—Frederick Douglass

I usually abstain from questions that ask me to strictly classify my religion. I am seminary trained, and I served as a Christian pastor for years, so I suppose I will always be associated with Christianity. But I'm very uncomfortable being called a Christian because much that passes for Christianity these days saddens me.

You could say that my religion is Native American traditional, although I offer this up with some hesitation as well because I was not raised traditionally. Maybe my mixed-blood heritage conveyed some Indigenous values, but I was not taught the ceremonies and songs and stories until I was a young adult. I needed to both reclaim and grow into that Indigenous world and into that worldview. I guess I'm just not much for labels.

One of the unique characteristics of a Western worldview is the fixation on categorizing and defining knowledge. I think this tendency to strictly categorize stems from a deep desire to control the world. Religion is one of those categories. Once categorized, a religion is then subdivided into histories and doctrinal affirmations and beliefs. If the religion is Christianity, then the first category is, Are you a Christian or not a Christian? Next comes, Protestant or Catholic? Then the categories break down even further: evangelical, Pentecostal, mainline, Anabaptist, dispensational, Reformed . . . and it continues ad infinitum.

These differences were created from debates concerning the Christian faith in the early days of creedal formations and discussions in centers of power, sometimes even to the point of bloodshed. Note: there were no wars of religion in America prior to 1492.

I was very fortunate that mentors and elders, early in my journey, were willing to share their understandings of religion with me. Maybe the closest thing to a real doctrinal statement I have heard from the lips of a traditional Indigenous leader is this: "God is the Great Mystery." He left it at that.

The Western world has religions, and that's OK with me; to each their own. But sometimes the price of religion has drained God of that mystery and forced people to join a particular camp of presumed certainty.

As for me, I choose the camp of uncertainty. I leave Great Mystery to be explored and humbly understood and known as best I can.

What words would you use to describe your religion? Your spirituality? What of Great Mystery pulls you toward it? Give a word of thanks today.

85

DUCK, DUCK, GOOSE

We are never happy until we learn to laugh at ourselves.
—Dorothy Dix

One of the strangest things I have ever seen occurred during my first visit to the Stewart Indian Reservation in Nevada, where I pastored for seven years. It happened just weeks after we had arrived there, in Carson City, Nevada. It was a cold, sunny day, and Edith and I were going for a walk with our kids in tow in the local neighborhood. We were just walking by the homes on the reservation, hoping to meet people and introduce ourselves as the new pastor and family of the neighborhood church.

The first person we saw was standing in her yard, looking as though she wanted to meet us. It turns out that she was a Washoe tribal council member. As we were making the introductions and starting a conversation, we began to hear this strange racket coming out of the sky. We all looked up, and together we saw a very unexpected spectacle.

Almost directly above us was a flock of Canada Geese, a very common sight for that time of the year. What was different about this particular group was that at the front of the flock was a male Mallard duck. He was frantically trying to squeeze in as the leader in the front of the large V of geese!

The display immediately brought on wonder, which turned quickly into hilarity. Edith and I and our children and our new friend laughed together at that duck's self-inflated attempts at leadership. It was obvious to all of us that there was no way this move was going to work out to the duck's advantage.

As an outsider finding myself in a leadership role in the community, I heard the message loud and clear: "Don't be like that duck!" And perhaps a second message of even more importance: "Don't take yourself too seriously!"

I sometimes wonder, What does the rest of the community of creation think of us humans? Are they laughing at us? Do they see us take ourselves much too seriously?

I learned much about humility from that encounter—mostly not to take myself too seriously and to always make a point of listening to others.

Find the things in nature that make you laugh at yourself. And what might other creatures find amusing about you?

86

INVASIVES

Immigrants and Native Americans have made our country what it is today, and if we've learned anything through these hundreds of years—it should be that we can accomplish more when we work together.

—Deb Haaland, Laguna Pueblo

One of the hard realities we face in this country is the constant influx of invasive plant species. When the Europeans first arrived on the continent, they brought with them not only their cultures but their seeds as well. Between demolishing the virgin forest and replanting new species of plant life, both intentionally and by accident, the settlers remade the whole flora of America such that it is now vastly different than it was in 1491.

A few of the particularly invasive plant species in the Pacific Northwest are Scotch broom, various knapweeds, and Himalayan (or Armenian) blackberry. In Oregon, various state agencies are tasked with eradicating invasives. Problem is, they just keep coming back. It seems like once an invasive species is here, it's here to stay.

On the nearly ten acres that we share with various animals and plants, Edith and I encounter invasive species daily. Our approach has been somewhat different than the state's. Our goal is to rewild parts of the land on which we live: to return it to wildness with native plants. Eventually, it will take the form of an oak savannah. But we also realize that because the invasives are now present, we can't go back in time and create a false landscape that takes care of itself. So we learn to manage the invasives.

All plants, just like all people, have a purpose. Although the invasive species are not originally from this land, we try to understand their purpose, and we watch how they interact with the native plants. If an invasive species insists on taking over, we have to make severe cuts. If, however, the species learns to interact well with the native plants and the rest of the community of creation, we allow more of the population to flourish.

Each plant, even the invasives, have their own cultural beauty. And we do enjoy picking and eating blackberries!

Although it will take much more effort from us, our land will ultimately retain much of the native character it once had. In some ways, it may even be enhanced by the newer species. Whether from another country or native, they are all our relatives.

Today, discover the good in something, or someone, you have always thought of as lesser.

87

CARELESS THOUGHTS

Men never do evil so completely and cheerfully as when they do it from religious conviction.

—Blaise Pascal

The Himalayan blackberry plant produces a wonderfully large, plump, sweet, and delicious berry. Pacific Northwesterners can hardly wait for the time when the berries are finally ready to pick so we can enjoy them in pies, cobblers, and smoothies, and especially right off the bush.

We particularly appreciate July, the month-long season of blackberry fruitage. For the rest of the year, we spend considerable time and labor trying to eradicate this extremely invasive species. There is hardly an area in western Washington or Oregon where one cannot spot this botanical behemoth.

The story of the introduction of the Himalayan blackberry is worth mentioning. Years ago, in Santa Rosa, California, there lived an unusual man named Luther Burbank who spent considerable time and labor ideating on his experimental farm. Pacific Northwest agricultural history was changed forever when Burbank opened a packet of blackberry seeds he had received from India. In that simple act, he unleashed what is for our region the Pandora's box of the plant world.

The Himalayan blackberry (actually originating in Armenia) thrives in extremely wet environments and in severe drought conditions. It grows in direct sun and in the shade. Its seeds are spread through bird droppings as well as through its own self-propagation. Almost anywhere the vine touches the ground, it sets another plant. The vines from the Himalayan blackberry plant, if not deterred, will easily take down fences and take over buildings and other structures. The Himalayan blackberry is considered a curse in our region because, if not kept in check, it roots out native plant species and replaces them with itself. The plant is, in a word, murderous.

As a self-made botanist, Burbank was also a follower of the popular eugenics movement, which was especially prevalent in America and Great Britain at the time. Condemned now as racist pseudoscience, eugenics was understood at the end of the nineteenth century, and until the mid-twentieth century, simply as "science."

The eugenics movement was not just a damaging pseudoscience but a rationale for genocide against all non-White people. The intention of eugenics was to eventually root out the presumed "inferior races" (read the "non-White") replacing them with the supposed "superior White race." From the forced sterilization of untold thousands of African Americans and Native Americans, to the enforcement of Jim Crow laws, to the establishment of Native American residential boarding schools that were often literally chambers of horror, eugenics was by no means harmless. Eugenics served to reinforce racism and stereotypes already present in the White American psyche while creating extreme, psychologically oppressive forms of self-hatred in Black, Indigenous, and other People of Color (BIPOC). Racism is very real, deadly, and alive and well in North America. How do genocidal theories and practices such as eugenics, and other forms of pernicious racism, invade our world? Blackberries can appear harmless too.

Take note of what you think and speak. There could be something harmful lurking behind what may, to you, seem "natural."

88

TREES

I think that I shall never see / a poem lovely as a tree. / A tree whose hungry mouth is prest against the earth's sweet flowing breast . . . / Poems are made by fools like me, / but only God can make a tree.

—Joyce Kilmer

Trees are not just remarkable to look at; they are remarkable. Full stop. Trees take the sun's photons and turn them into energy, life, for all to survive. In Japan, people enjoy a relaxing pastime known as *shinrin-yoku*, or "forest bathing," which is to deliberately leave the hustle and bustle of city life and go for a walk or sit and relax in a forest, taking in the fullness of nature as a sort of therapy.

There is something so primal that happens in our senses when we enter a forest. The trees begin to embrace us. That rich smell of decaying leaves immediately tells us life is in full swing in the forest.

But much more is happening than we realize. Trees actually omit a chemical reaction that we don't even notice when we enter a forest. The chemical aerosols from the trees benefit our immune systems. Not only do many medicines come from trees, but the chemical compounds inside trees create medicine for us.

Forests are truly medicinal, and they provide benefits no doctor can give. While boosting our immune system, they also call us to relax.

There's so much more that can be said about trees and forests: how they communicate with each other, how their heartbeats sound, the songs they sing, the way their immune defense systems work.

But for now, just enjoy them.

If you have access to the woods, go forest bathe today. If you don't, find a tree near you and meditate in its presence.

89

LITTLE DOT

We are shaped and fashioned by what we love.
—Johann Wolfgang von Goethe

An abundance of books and research have been produced about dogs and cats. The question on everyone's minds is always something like "Just how much do they really *know*?" We ascribe to our pets certain traits that make them seem human—and sometimes even more than human. We do this because they are important to us; they capture both our imaginations and our emotional attachments. How many dogs or cats have we as a family—and especially our children—cried over when they went missing or died?

Little Dot was a mixed Basset hound who was with our family for seventeen years. In a word, Little Dot was a sweetheart. She'd look up at you with her big droopy eyes, and you just had to love her. I don't think she ever lacked for affection.

In her younger days, Little Dot was an outside dog. She chased rabbits and squirrels, played with the kids as they ran through the fields and woods, and slept in a comfortable house on the back porch. Sometimes we would find her sunbathing on the warm cement porch with Cali, one of our cats, curled up beside her, and Ernst, our rooster, nestled in between them. What a sight!

Little Dot—named for a small white spot on her back—was getting up in years when we moved to a farm in Newberg, Oregon. While looking at the old run-down, fixer-upper farm we would purchase, Edith looked at me. She declared with dictatorial proclamation that bore no uncertainty, "From now on, Little Dot will be a house dog." I have always preferred pets to live outside, but I knew better than to make a challenge. Edith and I and our family moved into the farmhouse, as did Little Dot. We made her bed in the kitchen, under a tall coffee table, which gave her plenty of room.

Little Dot grew old with us. In fairly good health until the end, she remained a faithful friend, or really more of a family member, to us all. In her seventeenth year, she began to slow down. She would no longer go on long walks with us but would reluctantly turn around and wait for us at home.

One early summer day, Little Dot slowly walked over and laid down beneath a large Cottonwood tree in our yard. Just before she laid down, she looked over at me with those sad eyes, and I knew she was saying goodbye. I told Edith my suspicions, and we allowed her to rest there until the sun began to set. Then Edith took a blanket, wrapped it around her, picked her up, and laid her in her warm bed in the kitchen.

By the next morning, as we suspected, Little Dot had crossed over from this life to the next. Even now, as I write this, I have difficulty holding back the tears.

We love our pets, and that love is a gift to us even more than it is to them. How much do they really know? They know us, and that seems to be enough.

Treat your pets with respect. They are a gift.

90

ORIGINAL INSTRUCTIONS

There is not a pauper in that nation, and the nation does not owe a dollar. It built its own capitol . . . its schools and hospitals. Yet the defect of the system was apparent. They have got as far as they can go, because they hold their land in common. . . . There is no selfishness among them, which places them at the bottom of our civilization.

—Senator Henry Dawes after touring Indian Territory in 1887, describing the Cherokees

I'm happy to admit that I think the Cherokee harmony way is the way all people should live on this Earth. What I was taught of our Cherokee belief is that humans are suspended between Earth and *Ga-lun-la-ti* ("heaven," so to speak). We are to maintain balance, or harmony, in our world through our ceremonies and actions, displaying certain Indigenous values. Cherokees call this path *duyukti*, or *eloheh*.

You could call it an ethnocentric bias, I suppose—although it's not specific to one particular people group. Most of the Indigenous tribes in the United States and Canada have very similar constructs. So do the Saami in Scandinavia, the Maasai in Africa, the Maori in New Zealand, the native Hawaiians, the Ikalahan Filipinos, and many other Indigenous peoples across the world.

In fact, I think the Cherokee harmony way is just another version of the Navajo people's *hozho* ("the beauty way") or the Zulus' take on *ubuntu* ("I am, because you are"). I really believe that the harmony way, in all its many forms, contains the original instructions for all people everywhere.

I think, whether by divine decree or as human experience evolved—or maybe both—all indigenous people, everywhere, came to understand something from their interactions with the Earth: that living in harmony is the best way to live and, perhaps over time, the only way to live that will sustain us into a hopeful future.

All people have indigenous ancestry. All people are from somewhere. What about you?

Who are your indigenous people? What was their harmony way?

PART TEN

LOVING THE SEVENTH GENERATION

91

CHILDREN

Grown men may learn from very little children, for the hearts
of little children are pure, and, therefore, the Great Spirit may
show to them many things which older people miss.

—Black Elk, Lakota

Among some Indigenous peoples, the ancient medicine wheel is
used as a teaching tool for a variety of life lessons. The four colors change a bit from tribe to tribe, but this circle has become a
standard teaching tool among Indigenous North Americans even
when it was not used in that group's particular history. Most often,
the colors are red, yellow, black, and white. Among the many
teachings that come from the medicine wheel are the four seasons
of our lives: childhood, early adulthood, adulthood, and elder.

Because the wheel is not linear, each stage of life flows to the
next, even elder and childhood. Traditional forms of reincarnation
are not a belief among most Native Americans, but both stages of
life are considered especially sacred by Indigenous people. They
have much in common with each other. In both our childhood
years and our elder years, we need a degree of assistance from

others. Children generally speak from the heart, without mincing words, and they usually mean what they say and say what they mean. The same is true of elders.

Of all the similarities between children and elders, the one I find most profound is that both children and elders are in close proximity to Great Mystery. Children come from where? The mystery of such human intricacy just showing up in the world as a baby, as if there were nothing prior, is splendid. And elders go on to where? Again, this is one of the questions that almost every human asks, even if they don't speak it out loud.

Some Native American families are even taught that children, until age seven, are our teachers. Now that is a reversal of modern American thought!

We don't have answers to many difficult questions, but we do have the power of observation, deduction, and comparison. The relationship between children and elders is one of those mysteries. And sometimes wisdom can be found in our questions.

This week, go out and learn from a child. Use that teaching in your life, and then at some point, share what you have learned with others.

92

INTEGRITY CHECK

No [hu]man is an island.

—John Donne

When we look at our future, things look bleak. I could talk about the hottest years on record, the world's water supply, and animal and plant extinctions. I could talk about topsoil erosion, ocean pollution, nonrenewables, and even the Big Greens: those businesses and environmentalists who have sold out to corporate profits and greenwashing.

But I won't. I'll stop because you have heard all this over and over again. It is important to be informed about the world and to understand the climate crisis to which we are contributing. Yet the immensity of the crisis can also be overwhelming and paralyzing. Sometimes it is time to stop the influx of anxiety-producing data and just quiet ourselves.

While it can seem like the little you do in your own home and community won't solve the world's climate problems, don't become defeated. Don't believe that what you do means nothing. If you are doing something, it means something.

Light bulbs, laundry lines, and compostable sandwich bags are something. Drinking water from a reusable container instead of plastic bottles is something. Recycling, reusing, and minimalizing your lifestyle are something. What we do matters.

Most of us also influence others in one way or another. Children, students, friends, neighbors, coworkers—they are all watching how we connect with sacred Earth. Perhaps we don't even notice the fact that we are role models. And if, on the rare chance, you lack someone who watches you, maybe you can use a talent you have to shine a light, like writing an editorial, a poem, or a song to be posted online.

Even if you feel like you aren't influencing anyone, know this: you are a role model to yourself. It may sound strange, but it's true. We watch ourselves, and we know whether our ideals align with our actions. That's called having personal integrity, and integrity is a character trait that has great influence.

Integrity in this area at home gives you the right to step forward in the community for bigger projects, campaigns, protests, and actions. But tending to sacred Earth starts at home. From private to semiprivate to public spheres: step forward.

When it comes to sustaining the community of creation, which area of your life needs an integrity check?

93

THE SEASONS

The past is never dead. It's not even past.

—William Faulkner

I love fall. As the colder winds start to blow and the leaves begin to fall off the trees and compost themselves back into the Earth, our senses tell us to prepare for winter. If we have prepared, we can outlast the winter and eventually see spring arrive. The beauty of new growth, flowers, the blooms on the trees, songbirds serenading us once again—all these things give us hope. Spring flows into summer. The warm days of summer are a time to plant, work, and get things done. And then once again, like cosmic clockwork, fall arrives, regardless of whether we are expecting it.

Archeologists seem surprised when they discover ancient Native American observatories and markers showing how our ancestors kept calendars. Our Indigenous ancestors kept track of the seasons by placing stones and structures in a way that created exact alignments with the sun for winter and summer solstice and other important times of the year. I'm not sure why archeologists are so surprised. Just dust off those old archeological volumes, and you will see a myriad of references attributing these often intricately designed astronomical feats to so-called more ancient societies, who must have been here before the Indians. Because, you see, "the Indians were too primitive to have developed such advanced designs." Today, as difficult as it is for me to take seriously, the more popular version of this racial bias is to believe these remarkable places were produced by ancient aliens.

Here is a perfect case where the theory of Occam's razor applies— that is, the most plausible explanation is likely fact. When a civilization lives close to nature, it must be ready for anything in order to ensure its survival. Also, when our lives are built around growing, gathering, and hunting food in the correct seasons, we need to mark those seasons.

Of course our ancient Native American sites were focused on tools that marked the winter and summer solstice and spring and fall equinox. Those Indigenous ancients understood something we have forgotten: how to mark the seasons. They knew how to pay attention to what nature is telling us.

What grand season are we experiencing as a civilization? Do a casual look-up on the effects of climate change and set a plan to respond to what nature is telling you.

94

THE SUN

Each soul must meet the morning sun, the new sweet earth and the Great silence alone.

—Charles Eastman, Ohiyesa, Dakota

Many societies throughout history—from ancient Egypt to Native American cultures—have been accused by history of being "sun worshippers." Our southeast Native American tribes were referred to by historians and archeologists as the "sun cult." Although the scientific term is presumed to be without bias, I recognize a great misunderstanding that is present.

I have an ancient Keetoowah tattoo on each arm. Found in the drawings and pottery of the so-called sun cult, the design of the tattoo on my shoulder shows a sun design with other images. This is something I did in solidarity with my own history but also with my two sons. I share one tattoo on one arm with my older son, and I share another tattoo on the other arm with my younger son. When outsiders see my tats, they usually react with interest and want to hear a story of their meaning.

But once my son was asked, "Do you worship the sun?" The sun is a powerful force, but you don't have to worship it to appreciate its essential role in life. Science claims to understand how it functions, although I'm not so sure of that claim. Ancient Indigenous peoples have stories, songs, and ceremonies about the sun. What I do know about our own tribal history is that we did not worship the sun. We revered the One who was behind everything—the One we could not see but whose handiwork was the sun. We knew the sun was the largest of all the sky beings and visible to us regularly.

Indigenous groups honor the sun in different ways, thereby honoring Great Mystery—the force behind the sun. Most times we are happy to see the sun, especially on colder days. Sometimes we see too much of it, and we have stories about that too!

In your own people's ancient history—at the time they would be considered indigenous—what were their stories of the sun? Learn one and tell it to someone today. There's always more to the story than we realize.

95
WIND

The wind blows wherever it wants. Just as you can hear the wind but can't tell where it comes from or where it is going, so you can't explain how people are born of the Spirit.

—Jesus of Nazareth

If you want to learn to play the Indian flute, you need to listen to the wind. Stand outside on a windy day, find a windy canyon somewhere, or go into the woods and listen to the various modulations the wind makes as it flows through the trees. Each tree has its own response to the wind, and it changes depending on how the wind blows and from which direction it blows. Each tree sings its own song, and each forest creates a symphony.

The wind blows where it wants. We could not control it if we tried.

Perhaps this is a lesson from nature about our own lives. Like the trees through which the wind rushes, we each respond differently to the people around us and to other natural sources of energy. We respond differently in one group than we do in another, as each group is different. Each circumstance is different from the next.

When each person is respected enough to be able to share from their hearts, each conversation takes a different turn.

Every moment we share in the world is a sacred moment. The interactions we have will never be exactly repeated again, even if we are interacting with the same people. Savor the sacredness of these times. Allow them to flow freely. Encourage people to share from their hearts.

We can't control the outcome of any given situation but only respond to it. Let each moment sing its own song.

Begin to savor the freedom of your own lack of control of anything and everything around you. What illusion of control could you give up today?

96

STARS

Twinkle, twinkle, little star / How I wonder what you are! / Up above the world so high / Like a diamond in the sky . . . 'Tis your bright and tiny spark / Lights the trav'ller in the dark / Tho' I know not what you are / Twinkle, twinkle, little star.

—Jane Taylor

Few places remain where you can view the clear, supremely magnificent, unadulterated night sky without the bane of light pollution. Fortunately, some of these places are now protected as dark sky sanctuaries. Some cities have adopted codes that do not allow outdoor lighting to be pointed upward above a certain degree. These regulations help to preserve the view of the stars that remain in these areas. But even when we get just a glimpse of the stars on a clear night, we see how glorious they are.

The early Polynesian voyagers, particularly those who became Hawaiians, were at one time the finest navigators on Earth. The Hawaiians memorized the stars and their patterns and positions and then followed them to unknown places. They even crossed the largest sea in the world, the Pacific Ocean, finding their way using natural clues from sea and sky.

The skills of these early navigators amaze me. I am also in awe of the courage it took to leave friends and family, not knowing where you might land or if you would ever return.

An infinite number of thoughts may surround you when you are stargazing, but what I think of most when I look up at the stars are my ancient relatives. I know that the same stars I see *they* saw, hundreds and thousands of years ago. And I wonder: what were they thinking when they saw this star, or that one? I don't think it is presumptuous to imagine that they were perhaps thinking of me. They wouldn't have known my name, or my love for coffee and my disdain for large crowds, or my other idiosyncrasies. But in their deepest hopes and dreams, they knew I would exist.

As I look up at the stars, I also think about the future generations that will follow me. Will my descendants be here in a hundred or a thousand years? Will humanity have settled its differences with the Earth? Will we have learned that the way of harmony with the community of creation is the only way to secure future generations?

You are your ancestors' descendant and your descendants' ancestor. How can you be mindful of being a good relative to your ancestors and your descendants today?

97

RED-TAILED HAWKS

You see that hawk, he's headed for the Muscle Shoal. Take me a
week of hard riding and him . . . hell, he's there already.

—Jeremiah Johnson

I've long had a special relationship with red-tailed hawks. I'm not
sure when it started, although it might have been when I was a
young man during my many backpacking and camping trips in
the wilderness. Red-tailed hawks are more common than eagles,
and so you can see them more frequently. I admire them and feel a
sense of closeness to them.

On the day of our wedding, Edith and I were ready to get in the
car to head toward the place of our wedding ceremony. But just
before we got in the car, I looked up. There, circling overhead, were
two red-tailed hawks. It was a good sign!

A few months later, we were considering buying our first home—
a truly frightening experience for many young adults, including
us. We were feeling stressed and pressured by the fact that an hour
later, another couple was coming to make an offer on the house
we wanted. So we stopped at the gate leading to the pasture

of this five-acre parcel and prayed. When the prayer was over we looked up, and two red-tailed hawks were circling above us. That's when we bought our first home together.

These visitations have happened on many occasions, often when we are seeking direction over milestone events in our lives. When we moved to our farm in Newberg, Oregon, after building a nice chicken house and homing the chickens, I saw a pair of red-tailed hawks circling above the area. I spoke to them loudly, telling them they had our permission to take anything from the land *except* our chickens. The chickens would produce the eggs we need to sustain ourselves, I said, so they should stay away from them. I then walked in the house and told my wife about the encounter. "Don't worry," she said, "I have already talked to them." In eight years on that farm, we never lost a chicken.

When my time on this Earth is through, I hope the hawks show up, as they have so often. At my memorial service, don't forget to look up!

What bird or animal do you feel particularly close to? How can you improve your relationship with it?

98

THE VALUE OF NOW

You must not lose faith in humanity. Humanity is an ocean; if a few drops of the ocean are dirty, the ocean does not become dirty.

—Mahatma Gandhi

Does anyone really know what happens in the afterlife? I don't. I've been teaching world religions for over a decade, and so I know that many religions have various ideas. A surprising number of them—no matter whether they point toward heaven, or reincarnation, or something else—view the afterlife as giving us all new bodies. The more time I spend in the final half of my life, the more I appreciate the idea of finding myself as some sort of better version of me!

That this idea of a new body is present in so many religions surprises me. Given the last three thousand years and the influence of Platonic dualism on Western thinking, I am somewhat shocked to know the human thread of persistence still conceives us as a whole being: body, soul, spirit, emotion, intuition, all one being.

Although other models fascinate us, we as a human race are doggedly determined to be wholly human.

Since we are wholly human, it makes sense for us to be *fully* human. The present is where our spirituality exists. We don't get to "bank it" for our future. I actually have very little concern for the future. I do value our past history as a part of present cosmic orientation, but I don't dwell on the future. A linear worldview has limitations. It must have a real beginning and a real end.

Indigenous-oriented worldviews have no need to inject an extreme view of historic and future reality upon themselves or on others. With Native Americans, the past is an echo we hear into today. But the value of "now" is the critical moment. The future has not happened.

Besides preparing the necessities of life for our future, Indigenous peoples have traditionally taken life as it comes, day by day. Everything in our past helps to orient us to living today. After all, we only have today to be fully alive in this world—to be fully human.

How we embrace our humanity each day, including how we are going to live today, is our spirituality. Our humanity is exercised one moment at a time, one day at a time. That includes today.

As you consider today's thoughts and activities so far, would you say you have embraced your humanity fully? Spend the rest of the day living fully into each moment.

99

LONGING TO BE WATER

Life is long.

—T. S. Eliot

We are reminded daily that we must return to water.

Water is a dire physical necessity. If we don't return to water—that clear, cool liquid we all pour down our throats—we will begin to die in only about three days. If our bodies don't take in water daily, we become dehydrated, and both our physical being and our mental being begin to suffer the damage.

And so as part of our journey to reconnect with sacred Earth, we return to water.

Day after day, week after week, year after year, we thirst. For as long as we are granted breath—from that forceful first gasp of air at our birth to our fateful last breath when we die—we return to water.

We all return to water.

Eventually, we rejoin ourselves to the Earth through decomposition, and water finds its way into us again, and we in it.

We become the rains, and the lakes, and the rivers and creeks we so cherish.

We are water. Though I will likely have little choice, I long to be a spring.

What kind of water do you hope to be?

100

GOOD MEDICINE

In times of change learners inherit the earth; while the learned find themselves beautifully equipped to deal with a world that no longer exists.

—Eric Hoffer

Some estimates suggest that 70 percent of modern medications are made from natural plants. More than six hundred plant species have been lost to human encroachment and pollution over the last several hundred years. These two facts worry me. Why would human beings promote systems, structures, ideologies, and lifestyles that work against their own survival?

Good air quality is also a medicine. So is clean water. And healthy soil. Even a stress-free life is known to prolong people's lives. It seems to me that people in the Western world are working against their own self-interest—against their own healing—and against their own grandchildren's well-being. What will it take to change?

The only way I see such a destructive lifestyle changing is if people begin adopting different values and then living out these values. Our Indigenous ancestors figured this out—by trial and error and through necessity—so many years ago. These are the ancient values I have tried to communicate in this book, and the values that help us reconnect to sacred Earth.

- *Respect*: Respect everyone. Everyone and everything is sacred.
- *Harmony*: Seek harmony and cooperation with people and nature.
- *Friendship*: Increase the number and depth of your close friends and family.
- *Humor*: Laugh at yourself; we are merely human.
- *Equality*: Everyone expresses their voice in decisions.
- *Authenticity*: Speak from your heart.
- *History*: Learn from the past. Live presently by looking back.
- *Balance work and rest*: Work hard, but rest well.
- *Generosity*: Share what you have with others.
- *Accountability*: We are all interconnected. We are all related.

This is by no means a comprehensive list. But if we nurture these values in our lives, we will become more rooted in the community of creation. Begin working your way down the list and incorporating these Indigenous values into your own life. Search for songs, ceremonies, and stories from your own ancestry. Look for friends who align with these values. Then commit to immersing yourself in a new way of living.

Good medicine awaits us as we seek the healing of ourselves and of sacred Earth. The journey continues . . .

Remind yourself that you are part of the community of creation. Choose one or two of the values on the list and try to embody them today.